Also by Seye Kuyinu

Inside I Am Just Like You

Good Morning!

*Things I Wanted To Tell You In
Other Words: a relationships diary*

*Dates And All Those Things I Tell
You: a collection of short love poems*

this glorious dance

Thoughts & contemplations about who we are

Seye Kuyinu

Pressing
publishing

This Glorious Dance: Thoughts & Contemplations About Who We Are
Published by Pressing Publishing
Copyright © 2024 by Seye Kuyinu

Hardcover ISBN: 979-8-218-31376-0
Softcover ISBN: 979-8-218-34025-4
eBook ISBN: 979-8-892-98761-5

Printed in the United States of America on acid-free paper
seyekuyinu.com
pressi.ng

This Glorious Dance: Thoughts & Contemplations About Who We Are is found on Amazon, Kindle, Apple Book Store, Barnes & Noble and the author's website, http://seyekuyinu.com/book

1 3 5 7 9 10 8 6 4 2

To you, the same me.

Also for Milo,
Whose playfulness is a reminder of the divine,
Whose needless pain, fear and suffering
I feel daily. They are mine.
Whose loyalty and companionship has
taught me faithfulness.
Whose love for Cookie holds a beautiful story.
Whose life and certain death is part of this story.
Whose excitement when I get home reminds me
of the times I forget I'm home.
You will never read this, but, for now, sit!

Good boy!

Table of Contents

Foreword

My spiritual friendship with Seye began before we met. He had recently found his way to *The Heart of Who We Are: Realizing Freedom Together* and, after being moved by the book, posted a lovely video about it online. I refer to our friendship as a spiritual one because since that moment our exchanges have orbited around our shared love of truth—the truth of our shared being— with very little focus on the content of our lives: where we live, what fills our days, the differences that comes from being a white woman and a black man in today's world. The content of our lives is never ignored, but it doesn't guide our connection. Seye and I meet each other essence to essence and our shared love of truth shines through every interaction.

That Seye Kuyinu's book, *This Glorious Dance*, begins with "To you, the same me," says it all. In a time of tremendous division, we need bodies of work that remind us of the heart of who we are. We need words that guide us home. Seye's work does just this, joyfully. In this book, one of the things I love most is the sense of play Seye brings to lines of inquiry. Here he invites you to play as well.

On my annual summer retreat at the Whidbey Institute, Seye and I had the opportunity to meet face to face. There was nothing surprising about feeling the quality of his presence. Nothing shocking about the warmth of his attention. I was, however, left open-mouthed during our community share on the last night of the retreat—a performance by magician Kuyinu. It wasn't merely the tricks themselves that delighted and wowed the crowd, it was the way Seye playfully invited the audience to dance with him, to go on a ride, to be wholeheartedly engaged. It's as if he whispered to each of us, "Set aside reason. Enter the world of wonder with me. Come dance in the realm of the unknown. Together." We all joined him without abandon, and magic happened.

And now you can join Seye too. To fully experience his invitation, you'll need to leave your assumptions at the door. Seye beckons every bit of you into this body of writing and he longs to have more than a mere exchange of ideas. Seye's writing talks of "embracing uncertainty and expecting deviations" and his words embody what they point to. Because of this, you are asked to journey without goal next to him. For Seye, the process is the destination. In This Glorious Dance, he lovingly invites you into yourself and is a beloved friend by your side as you explore.

But be warned friends, be warned. To dance with Seye means to pull back the veils that cloud truth. It means having the courage to explore life and death and to not see them as separate. It means being in love with the mystery. Here, to dance means to have the steadfast dedication of a Zen monk and the heart of a whirling dervish. Most of all, to dance with Seye means to enjoy the journey and love the ride!

If you were hoping to stay small, rehash yesterday again and again, hang out with conditioned fears, and forever swing from seeking to resisting, be warned! And whatever you do, do not read this book.

Caverly Morgan
December 4, 2023
Whidbey Island
Author of:
The Heart of Who We Are: Realizing Freedom Together
A Kids Book About Mindfulness

Forewarning

Aha! Consider this less a warning—in the conventional grammatical sense—and more a primer for the journey ahead. Unlike a linear essay or novel, this book unfolds in thoughts and poetic expressions about life topics and issues that I find fascinating. You can plunge into any chapter or page without losing a beat. There is no particular order or rhythm to the beat of this one. One chapter may speak to you at this moment, while another may not be for right now. This book is not aimed at teaching anything at all. Instead, its goalless goal is to celebrate something that is intimately known yet beyond the reach of sensory perception. Something felt but could never be put into words despite my attempt to put it in a book— it's the ineffable Truth of all we are.

Friends often ask me what books have inspired the insight and conclusions articulated in this work. While I have read a substantial number of works(some of which I share in the Further Readings section of this book) that have ignited my curiosity and shaped my perspective, the crux of true realization lies beyond the scope of any written text. Written words, after all, are insufficient vessels for capturing the fullness of Truth that exists blatantly in front of us. Although I frequently cite Christian scriptures in this book, these references should not be misconstrued as the embodiment of the ultimate Truth. If you carefully observe and keenly discern, you'd find that even the raw, darkly humorous, and irreverent writings of Charles Bukowski hint at the same elusive Truth. You know what I mean if you've read The Last Night of the Earth Poems. I discern a unifying thread across diverse wisdom traditions—be it Buddhism, Advaita Vedanta, Christian mysticism, or Taoism—all of them point towards the same essential realities. To truly grasp this, one must look beyond the veneer of language and bypass the finger-pointing at the moon, so to speak. The focus should be not merely on what is being signposted but on that which the signpost is directing you toward —and to perceive this not merely with attention but with a profound level of awareness. There are signposts within this book. Words or phrases in parenthesis may be a reminder to notice this signpost.

While you can do anything with this book — you can gift it to a friend, let it gather dust on your bookshelf among other "to-be-read" titles, or use it as a chic coffee table centerpiece, its true utility lies in its potential for deep contemplation.

So imagine this: in the tranquil hours of dawn, you sit facing the rising sun, a steaming cup of tea in hand. You flip open to a random page and savor the expressive words that seem to flow like nectar. Alternatively, picture yourself nestled against the setting sun, wrapped in a cozy blanket with your significant other. Lo-fi tunes set the mood as you read passages aloud, sharing the experience. Well, it doesn't matter how you read as long as you enjoy it (or not).

But here's the thing! Every single book, including this one, is a manifestation of thoughts— thoughts that moved from mind to ink to paper. And so, thoughts that once danced in this mind inspired me to put pen to paper. These very thoughts will soon intertwine with yours, dancing in time, sparking newer thoughts, ideas, and perspectives, touching our shared essence in this very mysterious dance. Isn't that the most exhilarating alchemy of our existence?

Deny it if you dare!

Introduction

Something absolutely incredible happens when we sit still. I mean, *when we are absolutely still*, alert, and observant— when we totally observe all that is happening around us!

Somehow, we begin to notice things we never saw before despite seeing them in front of us all along. Oh! That's the main paradox I will be talking about.

We come to realize that our prior knowledge was less intriguing than reality. Isn't it absolutely fascinating that the heart beats on its own? Isn't it mind-blowing how digestion happens all on its own? That your body could signal hunger before you even think about eating. Isn't it fascinating how body cells grow and die on their own without you decommissioning or commissioning them by yourself? You probably have not seen yet that you don't control anything. Okay, you don't believe this. That's alright!

Isn't it oh so mind-blowing when we pay attention and realize that thoughts—your thoughts are happening on their own accord? Wait until we really see…really, really see that the thought of changing your thought is that— another thought— a thought about changing a thought! Tell me you're not awe-struck by the realization that thoughts are happening by themselves, whether we want them or not. They just spontaneously arise!

It has filled me with such joy and wonder when I watch animals in the wild just '*animaling*'! Who the heck teaches chicks how to break free from their eggshells? Who taught the day-old chick to run under cover when a hawk patrols the skies? Who taught the deer how to have sex? Did they have to go through any form of sex education?

Were there female toad gossip groups where *Fancy Nancy the Fertile Toad* learned how to listen to select the male toad with the *croakiest* voice?

Who tells wild creatures to prepare for the hurricane, birds detecting barometric changes and infrared radiation signals that prompt them into migration, and fast-swimming marine animals making an exit for the deep sea. When the bear goes into hibernation, it doesn't set an alarm for when to wake up. The mature female mantis never learned from its parents what happens during sex— how to eat the male!

What about plants? Isn't it fascinating that no single plant goes to waste? The leaves or stems that drop to the ground take up roots, and if they can't, they become food for beasts or other organisms. And if they don't, they become a valuable asset for other plants after them.

I know what you may be muttering at this point. If you're inclined to science, you may write this off as a function of evolution. So predictable, you! And if you're religious, you probably are rolling your eyes and marking the page with inscriptions of 'God's intelligent design' or 'God works in mysterious ways.' Playing into Douglas Adams' *Puddle Analogy*. And if you're a philosopher, you may blow the Appeal To Nature Fallacy whistle on this! But hear me out!

I want to propose that these may, in fact, be very lazy conclusions. Not that these viewpoints or conclusions aren't right. But look closer! Really look! Look real close, and you will see something much grander than words. You will see something so much more meaningful than what has been told to you in the form of beliefs or scientific documentation. You would find something so fascinating that joy springs out of nowhere to engage in this mysterious dance of life.

And in the springing out in joy, you truly see who you

are. Or should I say, *what you're not*? Ah! Yet another paradox!

When we open our eyes to see, it doesn't take too long to realize that all we ever believed was a lie. Okay, okay, not a lie because, quite frankly, there was no one trying to lie to anyone, and there has been no one trying to show anyone the truth.

It doesn't take long before we realize what we thought we knew; we had no idea! Enter another paradox.

Let's see, for instance, an object like a mug (if one's in front of you.) We think we see or know what a mug is. We may say it's a type of cup that holds liquid. But then, what is a cup? A small bowl that holds liquid? Then what is a bowl? The more we go, the more we find that the moment we put a label onto something in front of us, we fail to truly see it for what it truly is.

So, what is being seen, and who is seeing anything? Would this not account for the third paradox in this *Introduction*?

In forgetting who we are, we take things we have learned from guardians and society at large for truth without thoroughly investigating. When we take a colloquial component like 'time' as an example, we so believe that it is something that fundamentally and objectively exists. We believe it so much that we don't stop to actually *truly look* at it. We don't inquire into it. We don't look for it. Maybe, if we, in fact, found it, we could bend it, distort it, reframe it or maybe totally discard it. But let's not waste *time* talking about it.

What if we really looked and saw that all this apparent existence is nothing but a beautiful dance of duality? Good is not always good. Sometimes it's bad. Bad is not always bad; sometimes, it's good. So what, then, is really good or bad? Was Jesus hinting this when a man called him 'good teacher' and he [1]responded, "*there's no one good except God alone.*"

What if we actually ate from the Tree of Life, our eyes truly open to seeing the paradoxical nature of life? Suddenly we realize that what we think we know, we know not. And what we do not know, we then fully know.

This knowing unveils to us a dance of duality identical in its movement to those of lovers dancing. In any dance, there are identifiable patterns, some not easily noticed. But in every dance (save for maybe dance rehearsals), the dancers are not dancing so they can get to the end of the dance. The final step in the dance is not what the other moves were about. The dancing is happening for its own enjoyment. *One step to the left, one to the right, criss cross, cha cha smooth, cha cha now and* every opposing movement was required for the corresponding swing. Isn't it so obvious that life is just this? Even this sentient existence. Tell me it's not a profound thought when you realize that the moment you were born was the beginning of a gradual death. Or the realization that death is truly the beginning of some form of life.

[2]Ajahn Chaha, a well-loved Thai monk was recorded to have said this: "*As soon as we're born, we're dead. Our birth and death are just one thing. It's like a tree: when there's a root there must be twigs. When there are twigs there must be a root. You can't have one without the other. It's a little funny to see how at a death people are so grief-stricken and distracted, tearful and sad, and at a birth how happy and delighted. It's delusion, nobody has ever looked at this clearly. I think if you really want to cry, then it would be better to do so when someone's born. For actually birth is death, death is birth, the root is the twig, the twig is the root. If you've got to cry, cry at the root, cry at the birth. Look closely: if there was no birth there would be no death. Can you understand this?*"

My goalless goal in this book is to allow you, the reader, to enjoy the musings and contemplations here that I find to be profound. I describe this as goalless because, quite frankly, it doesn't matter whether I achieve this goal or not. But then, is it a goal at all? You see what I mean? Can we just have fun musing through this? Can we just have fun in this dance of life where we find that there's absolutely no meaning in everything? No meaning to life, no meaning to death, no meaning to love, no meaning to family. No meaning to career, no meaning to meaning. In fact, the wisest character in the Jewish scripture, Solomon, was recorded to have written[3] *"Meaningless! Meaningless! Utterly meaningless! Everything is meaningless."*

Ah! What does this mean? I hear you probably grunt under your breath, "That's a terrible allegation. If everything is meaningless, why life?"

You see, when we really wake up and open our eyes, we see that everything is totally meaningless. You discover that the mind is the only tool that asserts meaning. We can go beyond the mind to find that out of the meaninglessness of everything emerges something so beautiful, something so pure, something that is actually Meaningful.

In its beauty and meaning, we find a place for pain and suffering. In its all-encapsulating essence, we recognize ourselves as the one not separate from anything. We find that we all along had been misidentified with the content of our experience without seeing the objective nature of experience. We then begin to see the subjective awareness and then the sameness of both sides of this subjective-objective coin, the whole *whole*!

Each chapter in *This Glorious Dance* encapsulates the dynamic nature of recurring themes in human experiences, resonating through personal interactions with friends, clients, and coworkers. Furthermore, every chapter is accentuated with poetry that mirrors these central themes, featuring a mix of metered and free verses. This blend represents an artistic exploration of reality's formless and formed aspects, akin to dance's structured and unstructured elements.

Oh, it's just such a beautiful dance. If you don't pay attention, what you see is two people fighting. When you pay attention, you see two lovers dancing. When you pay even more attention, wiping the scales that blur your vision, you *see* that you were only seeing music and hearing visions! It was you all along!

You are the music!

8

1

Illusions

~~~~~~~~

"We take that which is unreal to be real and that which is real to be unreal." –Rupert Spira

Magic as a hobby has been a constant marvel in my life. I get to experience how spellbinding and mesmerizing it can be at corporate soirées, birthday parties, and intimate gatherings with close friends. But here's the twist—it's not the spectacle of the performance that really lights my fire. No, it's the awe-inspiring after-effects, the lingering emotional residue that's as ephemeral as it is vivid. You know, like that inexplicable frisson you get when a song profoundly resonates with you.

I can't help but chuckle when I remember that I have a cult of at least six people who are convinced I'm in cahoots with some dark forces. They swear I'm involved in diabolism, as though I've sold my soul for the perfect card trick. Absurd but also weirdly flattering, isn't it?

But it's not just the adults; the kids are equally mesmerized. Take, for instance, my infamous "light ball routine." Picture this: a glowing orb materializes out of thin air, levitating towards me. I gently grab it and proceed to insert into a child's ear—don't worry, I'm a professional. The plot thickens when I turn to another kiddo, instruct them to open their mouth wide, and voilà, that same radiant sphere floats its way out of their mouth. I cap off the spectacle by placing the ball back into a third child's ear.

Here's where things take a turn for the eerie. Sometimes, in the hustle and bustle of the show, I "forget" to remove the light from the last child's ear. And that's when the parental calls start rolling in the next day. Panicked moms recount tales of sleepless nights as their kids lay wide-eyed, fearing a luminescent orb is stuck in their ears. The irony? It's all an illusion. Smoke and mirrors—minus the smoke.

If these kids and their parents only knew the secret mechanics behind the spectacle. Maybe they would have noticed my thumb. No mystical forces, no supernatural powers, just plain old sleight of hand. The ball never existed; the magic lies in believing it did.

In my near-decade as a purveyor of illusions, I've found that the biggest skeptics—the adults who arrogantly claim immunity to being fooled—are my most accessible marks. Oh, the sweet irony! These are the individuals who fall hook, line, and sinker for my tricks. It's as if their skepticism blinds them to the art of illusion. Conversely, those who are totally enchanted, who allow themselves to be swept away by the spectacle, often enjoy the tricks the most. Relaxed yet lost in the illusions, they seem to be the ones that get closer hints to how the tricks were set up.

So, when the proverbial curtain falls, and the tricks are demystified, they are just basic mental maneuvers. The mind, in all its complex grandeur, was easily duped.

It's humbling, isn't it? To realize that our cognitive machinery, as advanced as it is, can still be hoodwinked by something as elementary as a magic trick. As such, it seems that in the intersection of the examination of belief and skepticism as to what was seen, the real magic happens.

Lisa Feldman Barrett, a neuroscientist and psychologist known for her work on emotion, cognition, and the relationship between the mind and brain, delves into the fascinating topic of our perception of reality, exploring how it may differ from objective truth and how our senses and brain signals shape our understanding of the world.

In her book, [4]*How Emotions Are Made: The Secret Life of the Brain* and in talks, Barrett highlights a long-standing philosophical debate: our perception of reality does not perfectly align with objective truth. This understanding is based on the fact that our experience of reality is shaped by our senses and the signals in our brain. These signals serve as the basis for our perception, influencing how we perceive and interpret the world around us.

Looking deeper into how our brain processes information, she explains how the brain receives sensory signals from the body. She describes how the brain is confined within the skull and has no direct knowledge of the external world. It relies solely on the sensory signals it receives, which are the outcomes of changes occurring in the world or our bodies.

One of the challenges the brain faces is what she terms the *Reverse Inference Problem*. Since the brain only knows the effect, it must make educated guesses about the cause. The ability to accurately guess the cause is essential because our subsequent actions and decisions are based on these perceptions. She uses this example: if you hear a loud bang, it could be a car backfiring, a gunshot, etc. Your brain doesn't know the causes. It only knows the effect, so it has to guess. And that guess is everything! It has to guess so the right decision is made quickly to protect the individual. If it were a gunshot, you probably would go into hiding, but if it were a car

backfiring, you might want to ignore it or reach out to your
neighbor to offer some help (if you know what to do). But in
the absence of crucial and critical information, the brain has
one source that it feels is quite reliable!

Past experiences!

Based on past instances, the brain generates predictions
about the future. It builds a model of the body and categorizes instances from the past to better understand and anticipate
what might happen next. This categorization is influenced
by sensory and motor features, as well as abstract patterns
derived from multiple sensory inputs. And so when it picks
up instances from the past that are similar to what's happening presently, it can predict what's next and what the individual is to do next. Barrett then suggests that when your brain
categorizes past things into categories, you have to ask, 'What
features of similarity is it using.' Whichever case, these sum-
maries and categorizations exist only in the brain; they are in
no way reality in their most authentic, rawest form.

This duality extends to societal constructs as well. Consider the example of money: we collectively endow pieces of
paper with value, yet these bills lack intrinsic worth. A $100
bill doesn't contain $100 of material value; rather, it functions
as a representation of that value, supported by a complex web
of collective belief and institutional arrangements. Similarly,
various other social constructs—be they governments, societal norms, or psychological categories—draw their significance not from any inherent attribute but from the collective
meanings we assign to them.

Recognizing the interplay between perception, imagination, and social constructs opens a window into the labyrinthine nature of our subjective experience of reality. The

mediation of our senses and neural activity produces an in-
terpretive layer that doesn't perfectly correspond to objective
truth. Yet, this realization equips us with the tools for a more
refined understanding of reality and our experience within
(and outside) it.

Now, let's engage in a few exploratory thought exercises,
the purpose of which I won't disclose—as a magician never
reveals his tricks. You'll need to navigate this for yourself.

Consider this: are you in the body? If so, where in the
body are you? Be precise! If your response is that you encom-
pass your entire body, ponder the implications of losing a
piece of yourself when you trim your nails. If you believe you
reside in your head, where exactly? The frontal region? The
right hemisphere of the brain? The left? Behind your eyes? If
you are confined to your head, does that imply your being is
that limited in scope?

Pinpoint your location!

Persisting in this line of inquiry, even in the face of internal dissonance, may be precisely what's needed to unveil
insights that escape our conventional wisdom. In fact, the
discomfort or confusion generated by this line of inquiry
might serve as an indicator that you are on the verge of recognizing something profound— a realization that has eluded
our collective understanding yet remains glaringly obvious
upon discovery.

What about the following trick question? For this, you
should sit quietly, get as comfortable and relaxed as possible,
and then investigate a desire of yours. When you have identified that desire, contemplate this:

Are those desires genuinely yours?

Close your eyes, sit still, and observe your breath for a
few minutes. Afterward, delve into the following questions:
What is the color of the desire? If it doesn't have a color, what

are its characteristics? Is it situated inside or outside of you? If it resides within you, where specifically can you locate this desire? What is the texture of the desire? What constitutes its makeup? To whom does it appear?

Tell me you don't already perceive the unfolding of a mystery that's not quite distinct from magic.

As I type this page, I am seated on a bench facing a lake where about 15 Canadian geese diligently groom themselves. You can see their focus as they preen each wing, move on to the other, flutter their wings, and readjust their feathers. Given their dedication, you might assume there is a conscious goal behind their efforts. Somehow, preening oil is secreted from their uropygial gland, located near the base of the tail. Using their bills, the geese spread this oil across their feathers, enhancing their water-repellency. All of this occurs autonomously, without conscious control. Meanwhile, the urge to urinate has surfaced for me, the writer, even as my body's biological activities take place in the background, beyond my conscious control. Isn't this all simply magical?

And here's my introduction to the idea that free will may, in fact, be a farce.

The concept of free will, or the lack of it, has intrigued philosophers, neuroscientists, and scholars for centuries. Still, recent research and logical inquiry suggest that the notion might be more of an illusion than a reality. While the unexamined understanding of free will presupposes that humans are the conscious architects of their actions, emerging evidence in neuroscience points to a complex interplay of genetic, environmental, and biological factors that predetermine our choices. And yikes! It seems apparent that they are, in fact, not ours.

Experiments like the [5]Libet study show that brain activity indicative of a decision occurs before people are conscious of making a choice, challenging the traditional view of free will.

Even if we shift our focus to quantum mechanics as a rebuttal to deterministic arguments (if you're so inclined), we're still far from securing free will. Quantum indeterminacy may introduce randomness, but randomness is not the same as freedom—it replaces one form of determinism with another, devoid of volitional control. Chaos theory suggests that minute changes in initial conditions can have vastly different outcomes, but these are still outcomes of a deterministic system bound by physical laws. Therefore, notions like "moral responsibility" become questionable under such scrutiny, demanding a reassessment of social, legal, and ethical frameworks.

From a psychological perspective, the illusion of free will is a necessary construct for an illusory assurance of mental health. The belief in one's ability to make choices is correlated with better psychological well-being, even if that belief is based on an illusion. Socially, this illusion might be evolutionarily beneficial, upholding the societal structures that rely on the concept of personal responsibility. Yes, it is still an illusion of free will. Please don't take my word for it, or anyone's word for that matter. Find out only for yourself.

While the belief in free will may be ingrained in our psychology and social fabric, emerging scientific, philosophical, and technological developments challenge its validity, compelling us to rethink our most fundamental assumptions about autonomy and agency.

Watch out for this evidence out in the world also: advancements in artificial intelligence and machine learning will eventually push us to revisit the free will debate. As algorithms become increasingly capable of predicting human behavior, the illusion of free will could erode, leaving society with both ethical and existential questions to grapple with.

And all of these have actually been explored in earlier centuries. Philosophies like Stoicism and Buddhist traditions emphasize the understanding and acceptance of things just as they are. This focus perhaps stems from the realization that our perception of control may be illusory. Accepting this serves as an antidote to suffering.

So, let's pause the debate for a moment. You could investigate this matter for yourself. All you need to do is turn inward to the stillness within and open your eyes to your own direct experience.

As you witness this unfolding truth, deny, if you can, its sheer fascination. Assert, if you dare, that it is not part of this splendid dance of duality.

Now, let's go deeper in our exploration of who, what, and where we are. What all of *this* is!

i am not

i marvel in the realization
that the universe
is the one alive and not me.
it breathes through me
even though i have no breath
it speaks through me
even though i'm unspoken
it lives through me
yet i didn't choose life.

it's fascinating to realize
that the universe
is as alive or as dead as i am
this character only a cell
in this mammothious organism—
this perceiving, being perceived by nature

can't we see that water isn't water
it only is called water
trees aren't trees
they only are called trees
the meadow isn't a meadow
they only are called meadows

check! examine that blade of grass
see that it isn't a blade of grass.
it truly is this unspeakable non-sense
where existence is
and i am not

a dance of memories

in a dim-lit bar, my memories
have spilled their liquor
haunting every corner of my psyche

they cling to yesterday,
those sepia-toned snapshots—
the laughter, the tears,
the could've-beens that never were.
a grainy film reel
looping in the cinema of regrets,
a theater of drama and shame.

as if it weren't enough,
they grasp at tomorrows
yet to unfold their wings—
as if the tomorrow
or the unfolded wings
were literal-- expressions that are
forever out of reach.
as if it weren't enough,
they reach for yesterday
and the day before yesterday
and the one after that
hoping some kind of time jump
would fix wounds and revive spent memories.

between these two poles,
the thoughts stretch
like a taut wire—
a highline over an abyss
where the present is but a fleeting shadow,
neglected and untraveled.

oscillating, these ghosts
of past and phantasms of future,
are in a dance that knows no end.

nothing but a dream

each step away from this very moment
is a step into the maze—
a never-ending journey
that leads only
to more yearning,
more grasping,
more thirst
that's never quenched.
and so, the dance continues—
an eternal two-step
in a ballroom with no exits.

but there are exits.
you can only see them
when you see this dim-lit bar
was nothing but a dream.

a dance of moonlight

you stand alone, yet you're anything but.
your hands moving in the air,
the air being your invisible partner,

it's the moonlight. it spills through your window
gilding your world in silvered hues
your feet barely kissing the floor,
your form an ephemeral whisper
between this world and
someplace more divine.

every twirl is an echo in the cosmos,
every leap a flirtation with the pull of gravity.
you're stitching a tapestry of movement
in the loom of the night.
there are no eyes on you,
 but you've never felt so seen.

here, you are both the dreamer
and the dream.

Foundation S2e10

gaal dornick:
tellem said, "the best illusions
    need grounding in reality"
hari seldon:
the second you forget
    you're playing a part, you're lost.

meaning full

we spend a lifetime
asking why something is meaningful.

that itself is meaningless.

on searching for wisdom

wisdom already exists within us,
no journey required.
the quest for it? an illusion,
a mirage we're wired to chase.
stillness reveals what words cannot convey.
in this silence, dualities fade away.
neither search nor its absence define us,
wisdom's embedded, it's not the fuss.
a theater of illusions we often perform,
yet wisdom is the quiet in the midst of the storm.

the world changes

maybe we can't change the world
maybe we never will.
maybe we can change
and then we will see the world
just the way it is.

and so it changes.

this glorious dance

music reverberates in your bones,
an unspoken language that
only your body knows
how to articulate.

you glide, a specter in the soft embrace of dusk,
your silhouette undulating in synchrony with your shadow.
the night wraps you in its velvet cloak,
stars twinkling like distant admirers.

each step in this dance writes a silent verse,
each gesture a stanza in a corporeal sonnet.
no audience to judge, no spotlight to blind;

it's always been you, just you
and the sentient air, a duet of existence.
form becomes your audience, your judge,
your mystery, your conquest, your body.
and you're identified again.

you feel the weight of your soul lighten,
as if each move vaporizes a droplet of earthly concerns.
for these stolen moments,
you transcend the mundane,

your essence scattered among the constellations.
you are not just dancing; you are the dance.
you're dance, you're also the music.

now, the illusion

our dualistic training and conditioning
of seeing ourselves as subjects
and the rest of the world as the object
is what blinds us from seeing
that time is constructed
by the human experience.
it makes the ever present now the noizulli.

darkness and nothing

darkness, silence and out-of-nothing
everything dances into existence
it's a glorious dance.

our gaze

not the world, but our gaze,
defines the labyrinth, the maze.
how we see shapes what we find,
vision's power, a construct of mind.

alchemist of essence

we see what we want to see—
an alchemist in reverse,
turning gold into straw,
treasure into the mundane.
but what if we looked

—truly looked.
and saw not what was projected,
but what simply, profoundly, is.
there, we transmute perception
into essence.

wings burning

you circle the light,
enchanted by its brilliance.
your wings burn recklessly
and so you hear the flame whisper—
you are not the moth,
you are the fire, the light,
and your wings burn
they burn away all illusion.

the beginning of the end

where the beginning is,
the end is too
and where the end is
the beginning also.

the beginning could never
tell the difference from the end
and the mischevious end
pretends like it's unaware.

but there was never a beginning
there was never an end
we only call it beginning and end.

the end.

2

Home is This, and I is a lie

~~~~~~~~~

"When it is seen that there is no person who has a life, our fascination with stories about the future or the past tends to drop away. Then what is left is this ever-changing play of consciousness." – Richard Sylvester

"*The world is in your mind. Your body is in your mind, and your mind is in you.*" It seemed counterintuitive when I first encountered this statement(and I don't remember where or how). "How can the body be inside the mind? Isn't the mind inside my body?" I could almost hear my thoughts objecting. "I can maybe accept that the mind is in me, but the rest? Unlikely!"

If this doesn't resonate with you, don't just accept or believe it unquestioningly. Doing so would mean falling into a cognitive trap that the mind often sets. Instead, let's critically examine the nature of our own experiences. Keep in the back of your mind what we discussed in the previous chapter, **Illusions**. The mind fundamentally shapes our perception of reality.

So, if you question the structure of this statement, good. Inquiry is crucial. Investigate your direct experience and

remember that your beliefs about the mind-body-world relationship might be based on social conditioning or intuitive
but unexamined logic. Suppose we can accept that our senses
are fallible. Why, then, do we unquestioningly accept their
testimony regarding the relationship between mind, body,
and world?

This is fertile ground for reevaluating our understanding
of the constructs of mind, body, and world. This reevaluation
could, in fact, be revolutionary.

Both neuroscience and philosophy increasingly support
the notion that reality is subjective. Every individual's perception is filtered through a unique combination of cognitive
structures, sensory organs, life experiences, and real-time
emotional states. This makes the concept of an 'objective reality' almost moot from the experiential standpoint.

If no two people perceive the world in exactly the same
way, it does point toward the idea that the external world
holds no inherent meaning in itself. Instead, it serves as a
'canvas' on which our internal states—our perceptions, emotions, and thoughts—paint their unique pictures.

And it's a dynamic process. The way you respond physiologically or emotionally to someone affects your subsequent
interactions and theirs. It's a feedback loop that further
emphasizes the subjectivity of our experiences. This relation-
al dynamic not only shifts how we perceive reality but also
physically alters our brains through neuroplasticity.

This is in line with several philosophical viewpoints.
Eastern philosophies like Buddhism have long spoken about
'dependent origination,' where everything exists only because
of its relationship to everything else. Even in Western philosophy, phenomenologists like [6]Edmund Husserl have explored
how *our consciousness* shapes the world we experience.

So, it's not just that the world influences us, but that we

also shape the world through our interactions with it, creating a co-evolving, intersubjective reality. The challenge lies in becoming increasingly aware of these conditioning factors, not just as an intellectual exercise but as a lived, experiential understanding. The implications are profound, affecting everything from psychology and neuroscience to ethics and artificial intelligence.

Consider, for example, the following distinction: a woman embracing both her child and her husband simultaneously is likely to experience the release of different hormones, each influenced by the unique nature of those respective relationships. While it's the same physical act of hugging, the internal responses can be profoundly different. Moreover, varying psychological contexts can trigger different responses as well. A hug from an abusive husband, for instance, may elicit a different emotional and hormonal reaction, even though the physical act of hugging remains the same. This phenomenon serves to highlight the intricate interplay between our emotional connections and our physiological responses. Furthermore, the mere act of recalling past experiences can re-activate the same neural pathways, allowing us to emotionally and physiologically re-experience those moments.

If your mental experience is like mine, you will notice how the mind fragments your world into the office world, the family world, the neighborhood world, the personal world, and the world of all these worlds. In fact, you may even have a social world that's different from the personal world. Notice how this fragmentation has no perceivable objective border. Also, note that the world I perceive, and the world you perceive are two totally different worlds (see the chapter on **Projections, Projectors, and the Self-confident Self**) Have you also noticed that while my favorite color is brown, yours may be red? What in our experience influenced these unique preferences? Is that not an attestation to these seemingly different worlds?

You still don't see it? How about this — a reptile sees a totally different world than you. Let's take one reptile as an example: the pit viper. They have specialized heat-sensing organs that allow them to detect temperature changes in their environment. This is incredibly useful for hunting warm-blooded prey in complete darkness. I don't think the pit viper would perceive the world as divided or the world as round. Or let's use dogs as another example. While humans rely predominantly on their vision, dogs are olfactory creatures; their noses guide them through life. Imagine walking down the street and not just seeing your surroundings but also smelling them in high-definition. Each tree, fire hydrant, or patch of grass is like a message board filled with information—about other dogs, animals, and even people who have passed by. This rich olfactory landscape provides dogs with layers of information that we can hardly fathom, making their experience of the world deeply nuanced in ways that are invisible to us. For a dog, the world is a smorgasbord of scents, sounds, and sights, all woven together in a tapestry of immediate experience.

You may be tempted at this juncture to draw a line between animals and humans, concluding that only humans can experience the world in its true form. Before you go down that path, consider this personal anecdote: I sometimes find myself craving another bite of crunchy, salted, and fried winged termites. Most people I know would shudder at the thought, but that's a reflection of my unique experience of the world.

Your mind holds the key to your perception of reality. Whether you experience joy or suffering isn't dictated by external events but by your mental interpretation and reaction to them. Your mental state determines if you perceive the world as a friend or foe. It creates a distinction between outside and inside, here and there, home and not-home.

Where, then, is home? Is it a physical or mental location? If you regard home as a physical space, what attributes of that space qualify it as 'home?' Is it the layout of your apartment, or perhaps the Bohemian style of your living room, influenced by societal trends? If home for you is mental, is it tied to the place of your birth? What if you discovered you were born elsewhere; would that locale still qualify as home?

Is home located within your own body? Consider death: upon seeing a lifeless body, it becomes evident that the body itself is not the core essence of a person. The implication here is that the world exists within you rather than you existing within the world. If that's the case, where exactly are you located? The mind is the only entity that operates within the frameworks of time and space, but the dance—life, existence—is neither limited to nor defined by locality. It's universal.

This brings to mind the [7]biblical quote I paraphrase, "You are in the world, but not of the world." So, where, in reality, are you? The answer is that you are home; you've always been home. The locus of your existence isn't tied to any physical or temporal coordinates. It's far more expansive, shaped by the mental faculties that interpret and respond to your experiences.

Do we ever stray away from home? In a way, we do. But that stray is only conceptual. It's only held by the mind. Let's engage with the mind in this exploration. Let's consider a physical home — your home. Imagine you sit inside that home, but a thought shows up asking for you to look for a home. Would that not be absurd? So you get up, pack your bags, and start searching for home. You search and search and search. You enter other people's homes, examine them for a bit, and then walk out dissatisfied. You then go to your actual home to rest so you can continue your search for home. That right there is exactly what we do. We leave ourselves to look for ourselves, tempted into the wilderness by our own 'demon'— thoughts!

I am reminded of the story of the [8]Prodigal Son. A wealthy man had two sons. The younger one, let's call him "Prodigy," was tired of the family farm and the daily grind. He went to his dad and said, "Hey, Dad, can I have my inheritance now? I want to see the world, live a little!"

Dad, though heartbroken, agreed. Prodigy took the money and ran, living it up in the big city. Think VIP clubs, designer clothes, and endless parties. He was the life of the party until— well—the money ran out.

Just his luck, a famine hit the land. Prodigy was broke and hungry. He took a job feeding pigs and was so famished he even considered eating the pig food. That's when he had his "aha" moment.

Back home, even the servants had food to spare. Swallowing his pride, he decided to return and ask his dad to hire him as a servant. But as he approached home, his dad saw him from a distance and ran to him, embracing him warmly.

"Quick, bring the best robe, put a ring on his finger, and sandals on his feet. Let's have a feast," his dad exclaimed. The older brother, let's call him "Responsible Rob," was miffed. "I've been loyal all these years, and you never threw a party for me!"

Dad turned to Responsible Rob, "Son, you're always with me, and everything I have is yours. But we had to celebrate; your brother was lost and is found."

And so, they partied.

The big moral of the story is that he didn't have to leave. He had everything he needed. The struggle and suffering he endured were totally needless!

It has been glimpsed here that this needlessness comes from the mind's tendency to take this very moment and compare it with an imaginary picture, thereby creating an illusory effect. It takes THIS and compares it with THAT. And so, THIS is seen to be inadequate. THIS is seen to be incomplete. THIS is seen to be less fun than THAT. So we chase after THAT, not really finding THAT because THIS is always here. This is always TRUE, and THAT is nothing more than a reflection and not the actual image. The chase becomes exactly like when a dog chases its own tail. Frustrating for the dog. It's entertaining for whoever is seeing this. Another dance of consciousness!

What fuels our dissatisfaction with our present state, compelling us to incessantly seek something better or different? The answer lies in our internal dialogue, in the thoughts that say, "I'm not satisfied with this," or "This could be better." Have you examined this internal dialogue closely? Do you see a pattern? Can you hear its tone? Upon scrutiny, you'll notice the thoughts center around the concept of 'me.'

But let's delve even deeper into this analysis. These are not just random thoughts; they are self-referential thoughts. They insinuate a division, a separation between 'I' and everything else, as though one exists in isolation from the rest of the universe. This is analogous to a tree perceiving itself as distinct from nature, an absurd proposition considering a tree lacks the faculties for such self-analysis. The same logic applies to the notion of human separateness. It's an illusory construct, a figment of mental dialogue that posits you're not only an individual but one that is segregated from all else, including nature itself.

Are you following along? Have you ever sat down to watch NatGeo Wild, marveling at the incredible sights, characteristics, and behaviors of creatures captured by highly skilled photographers and videographers? You watch in awe, commenting on how miraculous nature is, yet overlook the fact that the entity marveling at nature is nature itself. The irony is palpable: nature perceives itself as separate. The moment the mind introduces the concept of 'me' into the dialogue, it immediately segregates itself from nature, treating all other things as part of nature and itself as distinct.

It turns out that when the mind dissolves into itself, all distinctions vanish. There is no 'there' or 'here,' no 'then' or 'now.' There's only this present moment. In fact, even this 'present' eventually dissolves into a state beyond words. When Jesus said, "*The coming of the kingdom of God is not something that can be observed, nor will people say, 'Here it is,' or 'There it is,' because the kingdom of God is in your midst*," could this be accurate in its essence?

Let's do something totally and beautifully experimental! This particular one gets me really excited. If you know, you know!

Ready?

These words that you are reading— where are they? Are they on this page? The black here on this page is just ink.

Are they in your mind? Are they in my (the Author's) mind? Notice as you explore, as you search for what nonsense I am pointing out, notice as the mind begins to either agitate or relax into itself.

Notice as peace blossoms ever so gently as you read these words.

Where are these words? What's the nature of these words?

What is the structure of these thoughts?

Baby, you're home!

What can be true about the statement: *wherever you are, there you are?* Isn't it glorious when you see that we are always home?

Let's delve into some more thought-provoking ideas in the next chapter— *thoughts.*

labels

the paradox of life is
we try to make sense
of what doesn't need
to be made sense of.
everything is an....experience.
we label things too much!

and that last part
itself a label.

spirit and body

take care of the body
and the spirit will follow.
follow the spirit
and the body will flow.

where you are

like a snail,
you are home
everywhere you go.

like a tree
you are on solid ground
nowhere to go.

slave of thoughts

it almost seems obvious
that in order to be fully alive,
we have to be slaves to the moment,
to be engaged with what is in front of us.
very simple but easy to miss.

very simple but really difficult
to the one who is a thought.

the maker and the made

and so all our experiences
are a painting on the canvas
through which the maker marvels.

our lack of imagination
only hinders us from
realizing we've been staring
at us all the while...

the maker being the made,
the made, the maker.
it's the glorious dance again

no belief at all

it's hard
to comprehend
when i say
you can be
without belief—
no belief at all!

you don't even have to
believe this.

who?

who cares about the past
apart from a thought about the past?

who is excited about the future
apart from creative imagination?

infinite jest

giddy exhilaration blooms within you,
an untamed garden of joy and whimsy.
with a playful twirl, you send invisible petals
scattering through the air,
each spin a burst of vibrant color
only you can see as starlight filters
through your open window

casting constellations across
your makeshift dance floor.
your laughter blends
with the melody only you hear,
a symphony of happiness penned
in the ink of pure abandon.

like a pinwheel spinning freely in the wind,
your limbs unfurl in all directions,
leaving trails of light and levity.
nothing is planned;
everything is felt.

the room is your playground,
and you leap and bound
like a child set loose
in an eternal summer's eve.
for this spellbound instant,
you're not bound by earth or time;
you are the infinite jest,
a sprite dancing in the
moonbeam's glow.

the dance of self

the sun dips below the horizon,
leaving you swathed
in the velvety hues of twilight.

a mischievous grin flits across your face;
you are the trickster, the jester,
the sorcerer of this dusk-tinted world.
with a flick of your wrist,
you send imaginary sparks flying,

each twirl a conjuring of fantastical whims.
your feet skip and hop in unexpected patterns,
unpredictable as a hummingbird
darting among blossoms.

you play games with the setting sun,
daring it to catch you as you cavort and dart
through the dying light.
each pirouette is a wink,
each leap a laugh,
each spin a playful shove
against the universe's solemnity.

you dance not just with your body,
but with your very spirit,
in a performance that defies gravity,
reason, and perhaps even reality itself.

symphony of drops and leaps

you move fluidly, as if the rain outside
courses through your veins,
lending liquid grace
to each pivot and sway.
raindrops patter against the windows,
nature's rhythm section accompanying
your solitary dance.
your feet caress the ground
like fleeting kisses, leaving no trace
but an ephemeral warmth.
with arms outstretched,
you pull invisible partners
into your embrace,
twirling them through rivulets of air and fantasy.
as thunder murmurs its approval, you unfurl your body
into sweeping gestures—each a brushstroke
on the canvas of this storm-lit room.
for a suspended moment,
you and the tempest are one—a churning,
yearning symphony of drops and leaps,
each feeding the other's fury and passion.

symphony of drops and leaps

the dawn creeps in,
casting hues of gold and rose
upon your private stage.

you find yourself unfettered,
the first rays of morning
have unlocked a secret chamber
within your soul.

with arms outstretched,
you pivot and float,
carving sigils of joy
into the soft air.

your movements resonate,
a silent hymn sung to the awakening sky.
here, in this liminal space
between daybreak and daylight,
you are unshackled from the world's expectations.

each pirouette is a whispered secret,
each arabesque a declaration of self.
the nascent sun becomes your spotlight,
the chirping birds your orchestral accompaniment.
and as you dance,

you metamorphose,
unburdened and reborn,
in harmony with the rising world.
you're not capturing a moment;
you're becoming an indelible part
of the morning's first breath.

what is the sun

to say we are all connected
is almost as ill-informed as saying
this page is connected to a tree.

is this not a tree?
is that body not a tree?

no?

then what is the body?
and what is a tree?

what is the sun?
and what are you?

beware of nondual-speak

'be aware of being aware'
what tautology?
so do you want to be aware
of being aware of being aware?

beware!

isn't this how we got lost in the first place?
isnt' it all just—
awareness?

none exist

this moment that we hold in this instant—
this moment that can't be held in this instance.
when i recognized it,

i changed the past. i changed the future
because neither the past, nor the present
nor the future ever existed.

and there was nothing to change.

no within, no without

and then we see there's no within
because there's no without
and so the kingdom of heaven
isn't within.
it is here.
but not here
or there.
it's neither.

or.

3

The Dance of Thoughts

<><><><><>

"Let go of all ideas and images in your mind, they come and go and aren't even generated by you. So why pay so much attention to your imagination when reality is for the realizing right now?" —
Adyashanti, Emptiness Dancing

Many objects and experiences are fascinating to each individual. We have diverse interests. Some people love to collect cars, some dolls, some people antiques. Some people are fascinated with the collection of plants, and others are fascinated by engines. I am fascinated by the experience and mystery of thoughts.

I remember the very first time I noticed that I had thoughts. I could almost see the light bulb come on. *Did you see what I did there?* I know what you're thinking, 'you did not know you had thoughts.' We all witness thoughts, but have we spent time witnessing their patterns, incoherence, texture, and velocity? I am not asking about the enmeshment with the content of thought. I am asking if you have observed the nature of thoughts.

If you will, let us try this little experiment: Locate a comfortable chair and choose a spot where distractions are minimal. Close your eyes and be aware of those thoughts. Notice how they rise. Where are they rising from? Do you notice that they drift away— almost like a flame blown out of a candle? Notice how a new thought, like a branch, suddenly emerges out of nowhere into your awareness— in and out again. You might have noticed that some thoughts are reflections of other thoughts. Pay attention to these meta-thoughts, as they can easily remain unrecognized unless identified as separate thoughts. Do you even notice they are separate thoughts?

Are you uncertain whether it's a thought?

Notice how each thought could evolve into a picture. Perhaps, a picture of the past, a contortion of an imagination. Perhaps they are a picture of what you may call the future. Notice it!

Notice how a thought may present itself as a bunch of sounds or voices. Sounds that are inaudible to the physical ears. Do you experience the voice of a past conversation? Perhaps a parent's warning, a friend's harsh tone, or even your own voice as you recall a previous conversation with an acquaintance. Do you actually see that the conversation isn't real? By that, I mean it is not happening at this very moment. Only a recall, an imagination, a memory of what had once happened. It is just a thought masquerading as a past conversation.

Ah! Did you notice the urge to do something more interesting than this thoughtful investigation? Was this urge your own suggestion? What's even a thought of 'your own?' Was it a thought that had the literal content with the suggestion to do something else?

Maybe you notice a thought like, 'I have ADHD; this doesn't work for me.' Is that not yet another thought that's pulling you away from this? That thought says YOU are the one with ADHD. Who is YOU that has ADHD?

Where do these thoughts come from? Are they your thoughts? Or are they other people's? If they are other people's thoughts, do those people own the thoughts, too?

Have you also noticed that an emotion you're experiencing at this very moment originated from a thought? If perhaps you have seen that thoughts are not yours, are those emotions yours?

We will use thought to analyze thought here. Let's examine one emotion— the emotion of anger. Recall a moment when you were angry with someone and felt anger emerging. Can you notice that the emotion of anger didn't start itself? It started from a thought. Who put that thought in you? Did you really create the thought? Try that with the emotion of fear. Where did the fear come from if not from an originating thought?

Have you noticed how fear or anger replicates as you dance to its tune? When a thought about shame arises, and you pay attention to it, notice how it increases in velocity. More thoughts that amount to more shame or even guilt. And more guilt creates a contraction within the body, almost like the body and the mind are the same unit. Are they the same unit?

Let's examine a belief. It doesn't matter whether it's a 'good belief' or a limiting belief. Notice how the beliefs are just thoughts that are fueled by emotions.

"Yes, but my belief is true."

Did you hear that thought? Notice how much the thought wants to protect the belief— the belief in itself? Or it could be a good belief, like 'I am a good person.' Notice how a contrary belief could get your emotions riled up. Where and what is the thought behind that belief? Where did it originate from? So, then, what belief is really true? You tell me.

If you're continuing with this experiment, let's explore the direct connection between mind and body. Sit very still and observe the sensations in your body. Acknowledge that you can indeed perceive these sensations. Pay close attention to what is occurring within your body. Maybe you notice a slight movement in your hand or detect restlessness in your body— your mind's hesitation and your body's fluctuation. Observe the correlation between the mind's wavering and the body's subtle movements. Isn't this interplay fascinating?

Also, observe the fluidity of time and how thoughts fluctuate between a seeming past and future, often overlooking what's happening in this moment, creating an illusion of time's tangible existence. Recognize that the past is merely a collection of memories, while the future is a realm of imagination. Pay attention to the ambiguous zone where memories and imaginings intersect. Just thoughts!

Notice how hard it sometimes is to pull your attention away from the stickiness of thoughts—like sirens with alluring voices creating a picture of what seems real. Even though you know it's just a thought, you fall for her mesmerizing song. *Poor sailor! Even the bravest of them still fall for the voices!*

Are thoughts a bad thing? Of course not! Look around you at all the things that have been created. They are all the results of thoughts. Look at the lofty inventions that man has made— airplanes, phones, microwaves, cars, artificial intelligence, even language! They are all the effects and magic of thoughts. Even getting this book was a thought that led you down this path.

Could we entertain the idea that thoughts may be their own entity, just like a tree and the wind seem to be their own independent entity?

Could we see the total distinction between experiencing thoughts, being encapsulated in a world of thoughts, and being the observer of thoughts? Could we even catch the difference between a thought and other experiences?

What about desires and goals that I have thought about? It follows that there is nothing to achieve in the future if goals and achievements are merely thoughts called 'goals and achievements,' and the creation of those goals and achievements are created from thoughts. So then, 'achievement' is just a thought framed as achievements.

It also looks to me that thoughts about pasts that haunted me are thoughts that arise in this very moment. Perhaps there's nothing to do about them. But seen clearly, seen in this very moment, there seems to be *everything*! And then everything includes the awareness of thoughts.

Have you ever noticed that every word that's spoken is just vocalized thoughts— no exception? Spoken words are nothing more than thoughts with wings—lifted aloft by the breath of vocal chords. In recognizing this, the dialogue you share with others transcends mere exchange; it becomes a ballet of sentient notions. Ideas, unowned and free-floating, whirling through the air. Your musings are not solely your creation, nor are theirs the fruit of an individual consciousness. Every discourse is an amorous waltz, a symbiotic choreography where thoughts, made corporeal by voice, dance in intimate flirtation.

Here's a big tip: if it is experienced 'within you' and you can write it, it is undoubtedly a thought! Here's another big tip: Thoughts have nothing to do with you. That's a loaded statement, I know.

Does this knowing, this clear seeing — does this not open you up to the beauty in the experience of being this aliveness, this awareness that's full of mystery? Does this realization not open you up to see freedom? If we are not our thoughts, we cannot then be bound by our thoughts. Is that not somewhat obvious? Could this knowing be a part of the same Truth that sets us free?

Glory!

the puppeteer

i harbor myriad minds,
one steeped in logic's grace,
another choked in tangled vines,
one lost in outer space.

each sings a different tune,
from siren's call to banshee's wail,
each thinks it owns the room,
convinced its truth will never fail.

conflicting councils stage a coup,
each vying for my ear,
they think they navigate my course,
and yet they do
they think they're in control
and yet they are.
the puppeteer of a fictitious character .

they argue, rant, and bicker,
in tongues both sharp and sly,
not knowing that the trickster
is the 'i' that says 'i am.'
and yet what tricks
is the mind
not knowingly

to the perceiver,
it's just a glorious dance.

i have many thoughts

i have many thoughts
one is in my dad's voice
one in my mom's voice
one is of the stranger at the market square
that said i wasn't good enough
the other, of the crowd that
booed me off the stage.
i have the quiet thoughts
and the loud ones
i have the super-fast ones
and the one that's timid and insecure

the one thing each of these thoughts
don't know is that i know what they are
the same thoughts masked as different thoughts.

they don't know
that i know
that they don't know
that they are not that real.

yet they are from me,
consciousness.

i have many thoughts

thoughts are now just visitors—
not residents,
and my eyes clearing to see the dawn
that knows no horizon.

it's here,
beyond the chatter
and clamor of identity,
that i find the still point—
the epicenter
of a boundless sky.

this is not the "me"
sculpted by years,
molded by experience,
or dictated by lineage.
no,
this is the "i am"
unadorned,
unfiltered,
untouched by time.

it's as if the fog lifts
and the mirror clears,
revealing not a face,
but the very non-sense
that animates each cell,
each thought,
each breath.

here,
in this sanctuary of silence,

the walls collapse,
the ceiling shatters—
and i am unbounded,
limitless,
pure.

no longer a drop,
but the ocean;
not a flicker,
but the flame;
not the melody,
but the silence
from which all music flows.

eyes blinking away the mist of slumber,
gradually tuning into the frequency of wakefulness
i see that who i am
is not something to find,
but something to recognize—
an eternal homecoming
to a home that was never left,
to a self that was never not here.

and as this this unfurls,
like a flower greeting the sun,
i am reborn
into the simplicity
of what has always been—
a luminous emptiness
that wears the world
like a garment,
seamlessly stitched
with the fabric of love.

you, yes you seeing this,
are my love.

quiet

it's quiet here.
it's quiet here.
it really is quiet here.
only sound i hear
is of a field of pure knowing
unplowed by the furrows of contemplation.

no words dwell here,
only sensations—
the ebb and flow of a cosmic tide
that knows neither past nor future.
it's the silence between heartbeats,
the emptiness cradling fullness.

it's a sip of stillness,
imbibed in a moment's pause,
that quenches
the thirst of endless seeking.
it's the canvas of being,
untouched by the brushstrokes of thought.

and as this experience unfolds,
like a petal gently unfurling to the sun,
it whispers the ultimate secret:
that sometimes,
the loudest eloquence
is found
in the quietest corners
of existence.

it's quiet here
it's quiet here
i'm home.

every thought

every thought
wants to return
to nothing

like leaves to soil
or waves to sea

in empty space
they find their peace

a cosmic dance
of silent speech

scent of longing

rose petals on satin sheets—
each one a whispered confession
of desires unspoken,
and fears timidly hiding
in the soft folds of my mind.
these thoughts!

they are the delicate threads
weaving the tapestry of my soul,
these thoughts—
tangled,
knotted,
yet exquisitely intricate.

some are as sweet as the first kiss
under a sky ablaze with stars,
while others are as bitter
as love letters torn to shreds.
yet each one a tiny universe,
a small world within a world,
cradled in the palms of my consciousness.

and when dawn breaks,
stealing them away in soft golden light,
they leave behind
only the scent of longing
and the echo of a touch—
a haunting melody
that sings to me
until darkness falls again.

cartographer

i am more than sum of parts,
more than just a fractious crowd,
i'm the cartographer of mind's
diverse and ever-shifting cloud.

collision

thoughts colliding like billiard balls—
clashing, rebounding,
spinning in haphazard orbits.

they're agitated,
these frenzied mental fragments—
each one an untamed stallion,
galloping through fields of neurons,
breaking fences,
scattering the livestock of calm.

they shout at each other,
argue and bicker
in a cacophony of discord
that drowns out the tender hum
of peaceful musing.

it's a hurricane,
unpredictable and untamable,
these thoughts of chaos and turmoil.
they're the screeching feedback
in an otherwise harmonic symphony,
the static in the serenade.

and yet,
as i sit in the eye of this storm,
i find a strange solace—
the kind you find in acknowledging
the relentless turbulence
of a sea that never sleeps.

for even amidst this tempest,

th-ought to

this is how thought exists in the spacious space of the infinite.

can you truly see that each thought is like a news ticker, ever scrolling, always random. where is it that they come from? and where is it they go? can i see that there's something else that's present but undefinable? this white space in which they seem to exist!

boundless! beyond the bounds of even this leaf?

this too shall pass

a lighthouse beacon flickers—
a glimmer of something else,
a silent whisper that tells me:
agitated or not,
thoughts are but travelers,
and this too shall pass.

dance in luminal space

these thoughts
with jagged
edges
& round ones (soft
as a lullaby)

dance in the
luminal
spaces between
yes & no

they are
the architects
scribbling
blueprints
of could-be worlds

yet still
sometimes
thoughts drift
like dandelion fluff
on a breeze

going
where
they will
(ghosts in a machine
that's always dreaming).

let them pass

look at that! look as thoughts arrive unbidden,
like unexpected guests knocking on the door.
no walls to hold them, no fences, even.

they don't stay long; merely a fleeting visit,
a scribble in the margins of a blank page.
wild wolves, coyotes and praire dogs smelling food.

let them pass, like clouds on a wind-swept sky,
no need to grasp, no need to push
the scent soon vanishes.

though they claim to be of substance,
they're but mist, dispersing with the morning sun.
no anchors here, only currents that flow.

and so they go, one thought making room for another,
in the ceaseless play of ephemeral things.
in this still space, they find their freedom.
and so do i.

oh gosh, i'm not my thoughts
i dance in the space they leave for me.
oh god, i'm not my thoughts,
they appear and disappear from within me.
oh god, i'm not my thoughts
i spin and twirl in the grace that's given.

maze of mind

in the maze of mind
thoughts—
tumble & scatter

(spin
like
drunken fireflies)

eclipsed by shadows
or
illumined by sparks
of fleeting
what-ifs and maybes;

oh
how they flutter—
(butterflies with
no walls)

impermanent
as mist at dawn
yet ink their echoes
on the soul's parchment

a dance,
a murmur,
a whisper
or a scream

these thoughts, unasked
yet
invading

all the corners

of my
universe
in
miniature.

seize, cease, see

watch as each thought goes off
like a leaf being blown by the wind
like vapor to mist
watch as the opening
between each thought
shows you how there's
more to understanding.

isn't it just mysterious the mechanism
of our seeing and experiencing
and how easy it is,
how conspicuous this very moment is

seize this moment
cease this moment
see this moment

it is here
whether you see it or not.

oh descartes

cogito, ergo sum!
cogito, ergo sum!

"cogito, ergo sum," the mind's hallway resounds,
a cartesian echo, claiming thought is where "i" is found.
"i think, therefore i am," an axiom neatly packed,
oh, it's a fissure in the logic, a fundamental fact lacked.

no thinker behind the thought, just a ceaseless flowing tide,
ego's mirage crumbles, nowhere left for it to hide.
the cosmos whispers back, no division in its link,
but a truer axiom unfolds but what do you think?

self not preceding thought, nor thought birthing the 'i',
in the dance of pure existence, subject-object unify.
boundaries all collapse in awareness' seamless ink,
profound simplicity dawns: "i am, therefore i think."

4

Forgiveness, Forgetfulness, Oneness and all that's necessary

"To forgive is to set a prisoner free and discover that the prisoner was you."
– *Lewis B. Smedes*

If you are familiar with the Christian tradition, have you ever wondered why many Christians, despite being surrounded by Jesus' teachings, still struggle to see its reality embodied? In this chapter, we'll explore the journey of forgiveness, the act of letting go of grievances, and our inherent unity through the lens of the Christian tradition. As a matter of fact, we will explore forgiveness and forgetting through the lens of our unbreakable Oneness. I will also throw loads of rhetorical questions your way to spark inquiry into what's lying beyond the surface of our illusions. Using references from this tradition, I invite you to explore Jesus' words about unity as I paint them in this chapter, not just as metaphors but as a potential blueprint for experiencing deep interconnectedness with one another, even with those different from us.

What do I mean? Let's follow this narrative.

A *nobody* from this tiny town called Nazareth has somehow become one of the biggest celebrities of Western religions (posthumously)- a man known as Jesus. He was reported to have said several prolific things that have liberated some and confused others, pointing to truths only those with ears could hear. And now, I aim to connect with your 'ears of clear hearing'—the ability to perceive beyond mere words and surface meanings.

Clear hearing, as I describe here, transcends the literal act of listening(or reading in this case) but the opening of your heart and mind, a willingness to understand the essence of these teachings, which often challenge conventional thinking, awakening us to a deeper reality.

From the accounts of his life, we know that Jesus' counterparts were very uncomfortable with the proclamation of himself as one with 'the Father.'

What is this *Oneness*? And who is this Father?

In one account, he said, '*I and the Father are One.*' They picked up rocks to stone him to death, but then he asked, and I paraphrase, "I have done so many good things. Of all the good things I have done, which of them are you stoning me for?" They responded, "We are not stoning you for your good works. We are stoning you because you are blaspheming. You, a mere man, see yourself as equal to God." He replies, "But if I do them, even though you do not believe me, believe the works, that you may know and understand that the Father is in me, and I in the Father."

If only they could see what he was pointing to! If only

they could hear these words with the ears of *clear hearing*!

Towards the narrated end of his life, he calls his disciples together and then [9]says a prayer, *"I have given them the glory that you gave me, that they may be one as we are one— I in them and you in me—so that they may be brought to complete unity."* Could we entertain the thought that that passage and the following statement carry the same interpretation?

I have given them the glory that you gave me, that they may know that they are one as we are one — I in them and you in me — so that they may be brought to into full awareness of our unity. That you, me and them have never been separate.

But was this Oneness limited to his disciples? For many, this Oneness he describes is for those who identify as Christian; to some, it's for the religious.

In another account, Jesus, referring to the underprivileged and neglected, talked about how he would appear to everyone and [10]say, *"For I was hungry and you gave me something to eat, I was thirsty and you gave me something to drink, I was a stranger and you invited me in, I needed clothes and you clothed me, I was sick and you looked after me, I was in prison and you came to visit me."*

Then the righteous will answer him, "Lord, when did we see you hungry and feed you, or thirsty and give you something to drink? When did we see you a stranger and invite you in, or needing clothes and clothe you? When did we see you sick or in prison and go to visit you?" The King will reply, "Truly I tell you, whatever you did for one of the least of these brothers and sisters of mine, you did for me."

Is there a pointer here? I see one! Could Jesus have been showing us something that was hidden in plain sight? A *non-separateness* of himself from those who were less privileged from a societal standpoint?

What could he have meant when he said to his followers, "I leave you with this commandment …love your neighbor as yourself." Could this have meant that we love our neighbors because they are ourselves? How could you truly love something if you saw it separate from yourself? Little wonder Jesus also [11]said, "*If you are offering your gift at the altar and there remember that your brother or sister has something against you, leave your gift there in front of the altar. First, go and be reconciled to them; then come and offer your gift.*" Would I be totally off if I interpreted this as part of his 'gospel' of unity?

Peter, one of his disciples, asks, "*Lord, how many times shall I forgive my brother or sister who sins against me? Up to seven times?*"

Jesus [12]replies, "*I tell you, not seven times, but seventy-seven times.*"

Many people cannot comprehend this! "You mean if someone hurts me, I forgive them over and over and over again? That's insane!" Many people cannot comprehend what it means to turn the other cheek.

Is it any wonder that in the story of Jesus, he was put to death, not because he killed, stole, or destroyed anything, but because of his radical notion of unity? In this day and age, such messaging will still be called insane. Our rational, self-protecting egos quickly find a way to interpret this, "You can forgive, but you cannot forget!"

The etymology of the word *forgive* (*fragebanq* from Proto-Germanic origins) connotes *a giving away*, a *releasing*. If something is given away, if something is released, how can you have it to hold on to? Where do we store it to remember?

When we truly see through the *Eye of Wisdom*, we come to understand that the past only exists in our memories and has nothing to do with reality. Our reluctance and opposition to events are merely reactions to these stored memories. By acknowledging this, we can extract valuable insights about ourselves relevant to the present moment without becoming entangled in the narratives we often mistakenly believe are integral, much like assuming the wake of a ship is a part of the ship itself. After all, it's visibly joined to the ship.

We can realize that our narratives about past events are only a function of memory. These include the accounts of what *others* did or did not do and what they said or left unsaid. If we were to lose our memory, what grievances would remain against others? And how will we relate to others?

"I get it; the ego wants to protest and protect! But what about…?"

But what about imagination? What about memory? What about right now? What about the sensations that course through your veins, irrespective of those thoughts? Aren't those the one thing that's true of your undeniable present experience? Isn't it evident that memories appear in the space that can only be contained in this *here and now*? The event and the memory of the event are two very different objects! Somehow, the mind's amazing protective nature wants us to believe we can do something about the past by bringing memory into this moment, ruminating over what could and should have happened in that past experience. Do you see the illusion unraveled in this context?

See for yourself, observe how the present moment contains abundant wisdom sufficient to establish the needed boundaries, guiding you towards restoring inner harmony.

In another passage, Jesus [13]said, *"Give, and it will be given to you. A good measure, pressed down, shaken together and running over, will be poured into your lap. For with the measure you use, it will be measured to you."*

Maybe if we truly realize this, we know that there is no

one to be given to except 'you.' And there's no one that's receiving anything. No one to hold anything against. *There's no
one apart from you.* And this truth really has to be seen to be
understood!

For a very long time, I could not see this. I would have
asked, "What do you mean there's no one apart from me?
What about others? Do you mean other bodies?"

What are bodies? What animates these bodies? Are you
in your body? Who are you?

What do we do with this illusion of division? Oh boy!
Have you yet seen that we stop seeing boundaries and divisions when we see through the illusion of identifying ourselves as a body or a mind? No self and other, no this and
that, no here and there. *Pause for a second. Relax into that!*

Our sense of separation, which is by itself a thought process, projects and says, "I am(or they are) not good enough,"
projecting another image onto this moment. It says, "I can't
forgive them; don't you see how terrible they treated me?"
projecting onto an apparently separate piece of life. It says,
"How can I be one with everything?" projecting its sense of
a physical boundary onto others. It says, "At least I am better than these other *insert an individual, a race, a culture, a
group*." Imagine your pinky so dissatisfied with itself that it
asks to be a thumb. Imagine if your legs wished they could
be the stomach. Imagine if fingernails believed they were not
just a part of the body but the body itself. Don't you see that
there would be no body without its parts and no parts without the body? All are one.

So, what do we do about systems of oppression that really
are truly spun from a sense of separation?

We inhabit a world rife with conflict, a landscape where
binary oppositions fracture society: Christians versus Mus-
lims, Jews versus Arabs, Straight versus Queer, Republicans

versus Democrats, Liberal versus Conservative, and so on. This polarization has become so pervasive that neutrality is often misinterpreted as an alliance with the opposing faction. Understandably so. Each camp fervently advocates its agenda, often at the expense of the other.

Upon closer examination—especially when one takes the time to listen to disparate viewpoints—the stance of each faction can sometimes appear justified. From one viewpoint, we can see that it's a necessary part of our evolving societal organism. However, a larger picture emerges when we elevate our viewpoint to transcend dualistic thinking. We discern, albeit intuitively, a collective identity, a unified thought form that merely masquerades as two opposing poles.

To be clear, I am not suggesting that these polarities should be negated or synthesized. Indeed, engaging in difficult dialogues and advocating for the marginalized are sometimes not just options but imperatives. These actions correct apparent systemic imbalances, challenge entrenched prejudices, and create a more equitable social fabric. While we may recognize our inherent undividedness, it cannot be misconstrued as a license for complacency or inaction in the face of injustice. This undividedness is *Love*. Its manifestation also includes the courage to confront, the strength to speak out, and the resolve to make uncomfortable but necessary changes. In this context, *Love* could take the form of activity against structures of oppression—it becomes a dynamic force advocating for societal transformation. It becomes a mold, a shield, a *Mother* that gently brings new things to life from amidst the polarities. What I am trying to communicate overall is that, when observed from an absolute standpoint, it becomes apparent that *Love* itself manifests as duality to the rational mind and completeness beyond that.

When this *Love*, this Oneness, is embodied, we are able

to hold a position loosely. We are able to empathize with diverse viewpoints, knowing that each position is influenced by unseen forces. We are able to put up with anyone and anything. We are able to let go of anger, hurt, shame, and guilt for oneself and others.

"*To whom much is given, much is required .*" If you have ever been forgiven, you can and should pay it forward, forgiving others.

How can you forgive others if you haven't learned to forgive yourself?

How can you forgive yourself if you have not seen for yourself that you were never broken. It is a mistake to view our perceived inadequacies as who we(or others) are. Our seeming inadequacies often result from our inexperience in navigating the complex array of events and eventualities in our experience. These 'inadequacies' are thoughts. Thoughts have nothing to do with you.

In the story of the character called *Seye Kuyinu*, I have done damn awful things. You see, because I've learned to forgive myself, the forgiveness of *others* goes without saying; it goes without permission.

True *Love* does cover a multitude of sins. It requires the grudged to bring no sacrifice! It requires no repentance to be complete.

It means forgetting and keeping no record of wrongs. If there were records, don't those wrongs still exist? And if the wrongs still exist in any storehouse, was there really forgiveness? This forgetting seems like a tall order to some, but I pose it as a challenge to investigate what it means to 'not forget about wrongs.'

A more exciting challenge is to investigate who it is that could even hold anything against an *other*. Is that not just another *dance of thoughts*?

brilliance of you

no one needs a formula,
a set of rules to cast, a cage to construct,
to investigate the brilliance
and nature of our own being.

our essence isn't something caught.

love like no other(there's no other)

when we sit
when we listen
we hear it.

its the loudest voice
its the deepest depth
it was there all along
a love like no other.

when we stand
when we fidget
it stands tall, unnoticed
by our rumination.

it shows itself
animated in the forms
disguises itself in the formless
a love like no other

but there has been no other
apart from me.

on forgiveness & forgetfulness

what is forgiveness
if not the remembrance
of our own nature
our own tendencies

what is forgiveness
if not the forgetting
of a concept —
a concept called the past

and an embracing
of what's fresh,
and true now.

on giving

and so when jesus said
give and it shall be given onto you,
it wasn't because there was
anyone giving or anyone receiving.
it was because there's no one but the self.
when giving occurs, receiving occurs.

silence that sings

this is not the persona
donned like a well-worn coat—
patched by scars,
colored by experience.
rather, it's the unnamable,
the ineffable—
stripped of all descriptors.

a tabula rasa
from which springs the ink of galaxies,
the architecture of atoms,
the poetry of a heartbeat.

i am neither confined to form
nor free of it—
a paradox dancing in an open palm.
here, words retreat,
silenced by the eloquence
of pure existence.

a canvas painted with the hues of awareness,
framed by the stillness that holds all things—
the seer and the seen married.

the emptiness that's full,
the silence that sings,
the stillness that dances.
revealing not a world to conquer,
but a beauty to behold—
a life to live as a celebration
of the nameless,
the endless,
the one.

quick fix

when i'm broke,
i find ways to give.
when i'm hurt,
i find ways to heal others.
when i feel alone
i find ways in which
my company is enough
for itself.

you're alone

and so darling,
when you sit down with your eyes closed
your hands in a mudra
go inside
go deep inside
and notice there's no inside
just the way there was never any outside
notice the only thing you notice is the self
the one that's aware of this conundrum
the inside and out conflict
notice you're all alone
notice you're all.

alone.

eyes

when we talk,
we stare at each other's eyes
like the iris is what hears

when we listen
we hear each other's voice
like it's the mouth that listens

could it be the recognition of ourselves
or the sense of our separation.

miss identity

we mistaken our 'self'
for the cluster of thoughts,
feelings and sensations
the self experiences.

miss identity

the father and i are one,
in the setting and the rising of the sun.
not two, but a harmony sung,

in every beat, in every lung.
yet, words falter, equations undone,
in the space where all divisions come undone.

the father and i are one,
in the silence, beyond the reach of sermon.
here, the duality of language is overrun.

everyone, you

everyone is a full story of you,
a mirror reflecting countless points of view.
in each encounter, a hidden clue,

to the puzzle that's never quite askew.
so when judgment knocks, and opinions accrue,
remember, each character plays a role that's true.

everyone is a full story of you,
a cosmic novel, in every shade and hue.
in this infinite script, you're both the writer and the cue.

everyone is a full story of you,
a single narrative in the endless cosmic queue.
no one apart, but a universal tattoo.

loneliness

we can no longer
see loneliness the same way
when we see
we are not separate
from nature
how did we forget

oh, yes i know.
we fell asleep—
under the tree
of knowledge of good

and evil.

love's capacity

mistaken views of power hold,
dominance and control, falsely bold.
true strength dwells in love's embrace,
not a contest or a chase.

know yourself as love, the core,
not a force to settle scores.
in love's capacity we find,
the highest power, for all of mankind.

love's capacity

it seems clear that every war
that has been fought
came from the perception of the *other* as
— the wrong
— the stupid
— the bad
— the lower-than
— and the less-than.

the one side creates
the other side

oh, such a beautiful distortion.

5

Projections, Projectors and the Self-confident Self

~~~~~~~~~

"Our minds influence the key activity of the brain, which then influences everything; perception, cognition, thoughts and feelings, personal relationships; they're all a projection of you." — *Deepak Chopra*

In my coaching engagements, I enjoy every opportunity I get to have this conversation:

"Do you really know me, Seye Kuyinu?"

The coachee responds, *"No."*

"Do you think I know you?"

The coachee responds, *"No."*

I then ask, *"So, do you know you?"*

The coachee responds, *"Well, no."*

"So how can we know others when we don't know ourselves? Can we ever even know ourselves?"

I sometimes laugh when I read older diary entries of me setting an intention to "know myself." It's particularly interesting when I see people on the internet say they want to spend time knowing themselves.

The question we should ask is what exactly is the self. Who is *you*, and who is 'other'?

In figuring out who we are, we may need to examine the mechanism of our investigation. How do we investigate? What tools can we use to explore? And how true or accurate is our investigation? Can we come to conclusions that are stripped of cultural biases and unconscious programming? I want to think so.

In the investigation, the first place to start is being comfortable with whatever answer comes out of our investigation. Our quest for nothing but the truth will guide us to the right questions to ask. The reason why that's important is that, in more ways than not, whatever we look for, we actually find. If you look for a lie, you find a lie. If you look for truth, you find truth. But if your search for truth already presupposes the truth, how can you know truth is truth? This really just means we need to investigate the process of investigation.

I know this sounds meta, but I find that's the only way this search makes meaning. Suppose you were going to investigate the transparency of a medium like water. In that case, you probably need to use a transparent container to collect the water. But then you can't know the truth about that water's transparency without investigating the container's transparency. In our quest to know this transparency, we may be led to other rabbit holes that even address how you find the transparency of the container. When that quest for the container's transparency is done, it's easier to go through with the entire experiment: what is the actual transparency of this liquid?

In a 1955 public talk, Krishnamurti said, "How do you know what you think is true? And can thinking ever bring about the experience of that which is unknowable? ...How do you know what is true?"

Like the water transparency example, we must explore

the container of our asking and commit to accepting what we find to truly see and know who we are. That way, when we know who we are, perhaps we may know who 'others' are. The process of asking is probably the simplest but most difficult operation. It requires radical honesty. It involves the acceptance of what shows up. It requires loads of patience. It requires some level of insanity. Why insanity? Look, it's going to be a new idea for most people. And it's incredibly alarming to see that most of us never really stop to spend time examining the fabric of the most fundamental thing to our existence— our own existence!

So, what is this method of investigation? To put it simply, it is a process of self-inquiry! Inquiring into the self, as I mentioned, is quite simple. Who the heck are you? In asking these questions, we need to stay with the question, and whatever answers we get, we have to find the truth in the answer. Just like examining the nature of the container that carries the water in our transparency analogy, we have to examine the transparency of the answers, too.

For example, if the question is *Who am I?* The answer may be, "I am Seye". But am I Seye, or is that not the name my parents gave to me? If I were named Jeffrey, would I still be me? So, I guess I am not Seye. So, who am I? I am a black male. Am I black? Black is the name of a racial identity classification based on the color of my skin, which is based on the location where my parents were born, which ultimately is a body factor, so that has nothing to do with who I am. Okay, I am a painter. Am I really a painter? If I stopped painting, would I stop being me? No! So I can't be a painter. I am a human. But wait! What is it to be a human? Is that not the physical classification of this body compared to other organisms on this earth? Would I still *be* if I was not told I was a human?

Do you get the drift?

In going through this process of self-inquiry, we begin to uncover other questions about the search for the container of our inquiry.

Just like in Alice in Wonderland, when Alice falls into the rabbit hole, I can tell you that the experience of inquiry could get disorienting. It almost feels like a cognitive dissonance happens, a paradigm shift is experienced, and one's existing frameworks for understanding the world are suddenly up-ended. It's a fall that you quite honestly will never be able to climb out of. It's a fall where the familiar becomes unfamiliar and what you know as order becomes chaos, the unconscious becomes conscious. But don't worry, it doesn't end there. What emerges is terrifying but beautiful, the dissolution of what was held to be true for actual *truth*. And that truth itself cannot be defined.

From here on, as you look at the fabric of our perception, all you see is you. You find it was always that way.

But note, the quality of the answer is dependent on the quality of the question. And the answer comes only when you ask sincerely. *Ask and it will be given unto you.*

In her book, [14]*The Heart of Who We Are*, Caverly Morgan has an exercise called *Being With, Writing From.*

She invites the reader to find a way to spend time out-doors, being fully present in the surroundings. The reader is then asked to identify an object that captures their attention. Using all senses to examine the object, the reader is asked to feel its texture and its weight and observe how light interacts with it. You sit and grammatically engage with the object, ignoring distractions. In a stream-of-consciousness mode, you write about the object forgetting rules and accuracy. You write as if you are the object going beyond description to explore how the object might perceive its own existence and its own interactions with its surroundings. The reader is asked to include a sentence starting with 'I feel...' to delve into its emotional or intrinsic essence. When unhurried, this engaging exercise reveals insights and details that a distracted or hurried mind would overlook. But more so, Caverly doesn't tell you what to expect, and so when I conducted this exercise, I almost fell out of my chair when my writing about a random fallen tree branch revealed something so powerful.

I challenge you to try this exercise for yourself. It should only take about 15 minutes. What did you discover if you did this exercise as instructed? Like me, did you almost fall off your seat when you realized what happened?

In Don Miguel Ruiz's book, [15]*The Four Agreements*, he cautions, "*Don't take anything personally. Nothing others do is because of you. What others say and do is a projection of their own reality, their own dream. When you are immune to the opinions and actions of others, you won't be the victim of needless suffering.*" But why could there be truth in this statement? Is it not evident that our assumptions and conclusions of others are something intimately understood? The person who you dislike because they talk too much. Remember that person? What is it about the *talking too much* that makes you irritated?

Remember that acquaintance or friend you've judged as unintelligent? The one you gossip about? What exactly is it that you find lacking in this person? Could you delve deeper into your perception? When you formed this opinion, were there other factors at play—familiar patterns or past experiences that resonate with you? What could be the underlying cause for your judgment?

Have you ever reflected on how dysfunctional the world seems? How fraught with dishonesty and chaos does it appear to be? What does this perspective indicate about your own mindset? Intriguingly, have you noticed that others might perceive the complete opposite of what you see? Could the fault lie with them —or perhaps with you or even me?

I'm not suggesting that the world is broken or whole, chaotic or orderly. I'm urging us to pause, take a moment, and scrutinize the lenses and filters through which we perceive our reality. It turns out that when we remove these filters, we can move beyond simple dichotomies of good and evil. We will see Reality just as it is. What is seen when Reality is unveiled isn't seen in colors. What is heard when Reality reveals itself isn't reverberated through the ears. What is perceived when Reality is tasted turns out not to be from the fruit of the tree of knowledge of Good and Evil— the one God asked Adam and Eve not to eat out of. It is revealed that the Tree of Life becomes the one. A confidence emerges, one that's not running away from God because you're naked. But one that stands with God, as God in true open transparency. [16]*For Nothing in all creation could ever be hidden from God's. Everything is uncovered and laid bare.*

This confidence clearly sees that self-development is an illusion as it only develops and polishes something illusory. That confidence sees clearly that a lack of confidence is just a thought appearing now. When seen through, a colorless, spacious, luminous mystery is revealed. Projection becomes the refraction of that light through the mind's magnetizing and polarizing function. When this is seen through, it becomes all fun and games. It becomes like a dance— for its own enjoyment.

Invite *what is*. See it. Truly *see it*.

masks

detach from traits that bind or free,
find clarity in vast identity.
not just a wave in temporal play,
but the ocean's expanse, night and day.

let go the masks, both small and grand,
see clearly where your true self stands.
in the whole ocean's encompassing tide,
unlimited, where true self abide.

self-development

i now find
that self-development is a waste of time
a polishing of the illusory self

jungian approach

in approaching change
from a jungian approach,
we focus so much on reflections
and then the shadow self.
but we don't spend enough time
investigating the nature of that
that casts the shadow
or do we?

you still are

notice this
or sit with this page.

what comes to you when you complete these?

i am ___
i am a ___

the details don't matter.

for now, sit with the feeling of that.
see how the answer you give names
a feature or a thing you do or value.

now remove whatever comes after the word *am*.

let the end of the sentence just float away
into the breeze of forgetting.

what remains. sit with that!

notice how vast it is,
how vast you are.

notice how still the center is.
notice you still are.

notice.
sit with it.

you still are.

projection

could projection be the mind
assertanining certainty
about another mind

could curiosity be the antidote

solomon

so, this guy writes a book
about meaninglessness,
then we archive the book
and want to give it meaning.

or we disregard it
because we are looking
for meaning.

window seal

all along i had been looking
at the dust in the window
and not the beauty of the sun.

meaningful aliveness

when you pause to rest
in the meaning of being alive,
then you begin to live.
it is the meaning of life.

meaning doesn't lie in things.
meaning lies in you
inside you, where there's no outside.

judging the other you

sir,
it's incredible how quick we are
to place judgement on others
when all we know is an infinitesimal part
of who they are.

yet, we forget our perception
is clouded by our own flaws.
in so doing we make descriptions
based on our limited vocabulary.
wake up, ma'am.

who is responsible?

their reaction is not theirs
your counter reaction is not yours
if that's true, let's find the culprit.
maybe they are just happening in you.

you still are

walls we build, all in the mind,
limits set, by thoughts confined.
human essence, a sprawling range,
yet we're caged by the perfect, a self-made stranger.

in mental constructs, we dwell and roam,
losing sight of an expansive home.
perfection's the lock, but the key's in hand,
break the cycle, let your spirit expand.

freedom's found when limits are scanned.

again,
limitations are only constructed
by a limited mind

the identity is restricted only by perfection

stepped out

you hear about being in the present moment?
like were you ever out of this present moment?
wake up!

6

Anxiety

~~~~~~~~

"The truth is that there is no actual stress or anxiety in the world; it's your thoughts that create these false beliefs. You can't package stress, touch it, or see it. There are only people engaged in stressful thinking" — Wayne Dyer

I understand intimately the debilitating grip of anxiety. This condition afflicts approximately 31.1% of Americans at some point in their lives. The memory of an anxiety-induced panic attack comes to me right now. It was my final year of college when I discovered that I had failed multiple courses, thereby jeopardizing my chances of graduation. Desperate for a reprieve, I sought to appeal to my professors, clinging to the belief that my exams had been graded erroneously.

Navigating the labyrinthine bureaucracy of my institution proved to be an exercise in futility. The Head of the Department displayed a marked disinterest in engaging with me, while my project supervisor was swamped with year-end responsibilities. I was not alone in this predicament; a lot of my classmates were in this same situation. We would often congregate in staff areas, scouring for any insights or advice that could extricate us from this situation. This was no

ordinary department at the University of Ilorin; this was the
Faculty of Medical Sciences, a faculty known for its contro-
versial operational procedures.

When the list of graduating students was published, the
absence of my name felt like a visceral blow. I was consumed
by thoughts of the shame and disappointment I would inflict
upon my family. Having invested nearly six years in pursuit
of this degree and having lost my father just a year prior, the
weight of my failure felt unbearable. How could I face my
mother under these circumstances? How could I face the rest
of my classmates, who I perceived had the impression that I
was brainier than they were?

Panic!

I dodged my mom's calls for days, paralyzed by the dread
of disclosing this unfortunate news.

As my avoidance behavior escalated, I found myself
shunning friends, classmates, and even my own family. In
any interaction, words like 'result,' 'graduation,' or 'home'
triggered palpitations so severe that when a text message
from my mother broke through my wall of denial, I nearly
fainted.

In fact, at some point in my despair, I found myself
praying to God for madness as an escape from the pain, the
shame, and the anxiety not only enveloped me but had come
to bunk with me. I preferred a quick death to the shame I was
thinking I would face. My imagination ran rampant, conjuring images of homelessness as my peers ascended to presti-
gious roles as doctors, medical administrators, and surgeons.
Food lost its flavor, and I sought solace in the excessive
consumption of soda. At some point, I was drinking about 6
liters of Coca-Cola daily, rationalizing that it was a lesser evil
compared to alcoholism.

This particular event in my life marked the inception of a series of anxiety-inducing events, lies, and cover-ups that would unfold in the story of the life of this character, Seye. At the same time, these experiences have imparted invaluable lessons within the frame of its story.

Even as I write this, I am in the throws of what the *imagined story* will claim to be a potentially 'life-altering' process in one of my closest relationships- patterns I have seen play out in how these are dealt with in the different scenarios, whether in an unexpected medical diagnoses, relationship turmoils, and financial instability.

These imagined stories are what anxiety really is.

Anxiety has the pernicious ability to obscure our perception, making us feel isolated and disconnected from others. It's a felt sense of separation. In that disconnection, we tend to be fixated mentally in a world that tests all the possible assumptions of ills happening to us. Isn't it crazy that we can live in two conceptual worlds simultaneously? One imagined in this moment and the other world where the imagination is actually happening? We have perfected this process over time so that our version of reality exists in the mind while actual *reality*, reality that's not different from *what is* can no longer be seen.

Anxiety is often nothing more than a manifestation of our vivid, untamed imagination. The imagination is propelled by thought forms. When we are able to shift our attention from the imagined to the real, we are able to perceive the different textures of both worlds. The real world, the one that's here and now, has a concreteness to it. It is the world in which sensations are noticed more intensely. We are aware of sight; we are in touch with smell, with taste, and with touch. The sixth sense, the mind, we are also aware of as it either associates meaning with what the other five senses are perceiving or takes us to a dream world where things are falling apart, even though nothing is falling apart. It takes us to a world where things are not perfect when, in fact, perfection will always be an illusion. It takes us into a world where imagination tries to protect us from impending doom. Yet, imagination is never able to deliver on its promise. The 'voices in our heads' then become the most fascinating thing, not the content the voices point to. Once you see the distinction, you cannot unsee it.

Standing in a circle, we were given a pen and a small piece of paper. I was familiar with this exercise. I'd done this before. I first carried out this exercise in my journal as instructed in Caverly Morgan's book, *The Heart of Who We Are*. However, doing it with 22 people I was meeting for the first time filled me with anticipation. And guess what? Caverly herself was facilitating this exercise! I'd read stories about this exercise as they were conducted in her "Peace in Schools" curriculum, and now I was about to see it live and in person.

On the paper, we had to write down the negative self-talk that played in our minds and the results and impacts of those thoughts. For example, if you write, "People are not interested in what I have to say," you may write the impact, "My voice is not included in group decisions." Or you may write, "I'm such a lousy father — missed opportunities to genuinely listen to my daughter."

After we scribbled down our thoughts, we crumpled the papers into little balls, turned our backs, and tossed them into the middle of the circle. We each then picked up a crumpled note. We didn't know whose *inner critic* we would read aloud.

The note I picked up hit me hard. I choked up with tears.

The person wrote about how inadequate they felt about their life. I had witnessed the same thoughts in my own life. As we took turns reading the notes, pausing to recognize the familiarity this echoed, you could literally feel the air being sucked out of the room. You could see it in everyone's eyes as tears formed.

Just like what we did in this session, in her book, Caverly encourages the reader to inquire into the illusory nature of the negative self-talk with a few questions, allowing yourself to be like a scientist of the self. You would begin to realize how illusory the voice is. You could ask questions like:

What is this voice?
What is the impact of believing this voice?
Is this voice mine?
Am I this voice?
Who am I without this internal conversation?

Only recently did I grasp the distinction between being subsumed by the content of our experiences and standing as the observer aware of them. I liken it to watching an intense thriller; the protagonist is unaware of the bad guy hiding in the corner, and you tense in your seat, hoping he sees the intruder. Forgetting that you are safe, that the popcorn bowl on your coffee table is more real than the projected story, the characters on screen are merely actors who have long since moved on.

But what about the real feelings and emotions that accompany an episode of anxiety? I have learned to allow those emotions to be as they are and the stories we let go of by surrendering. But how can we just let go and surrender?

The common phrase "I have anxiety" merits scrutiny for its potentially misleading implications. The verb "have" suggests possession, which subtly reinforces the idea that anxiety is an inherent aspect of one's identity. I propose that this linguistic pitfall may influence perception and perpetuate the issue. A more precise framing might be "I experience sensations of anxiety," which implies that anxiety is not an embedded trait but a transient state. Recognizing this detachment between the self and the sensation paves the way for a crucial cognitive shift.

Understanding these sensations as fleeting experiences can cultivate a sense of detachment. This detachment allows us to view these experiences for what they are: temporary and non-defining sensations that ebb and flow. Acknowledging their transience liberates us from being emotionally held captive by them. It is at this juncture that surrender becomes viable. This surrender facilitates a natural course for these sensations to traverse the body unimpeded by mental resistance. Consequently, we discern that these sensations, once perceived as overpowering, are indeed harmless. The psychological grip loosens, enabling a more balanced mental state.

I sat at a cafe with my friend, totally lost in the wonder of existence. "Are you okay?" she asked. I told her I was okay and expressed how I was feeling. From the perspective of awareness, there was the experience of thoughts happening, the movement of individuals, cars passing by, and trees blowing.

There was blood flowing through the veins of this body, the churning happening in the stomach. And so I blurted out how beautiful life was.

"It's so easy for you to say that! You're not going through a lot of physical illness," she responded. She went on to tell me about a family member who was going through a physical ailment that was affecting her relationship with her kids.

I explained how this perspective advocates for a nuanced

understanding of life's complexities. On the one hand, there is the realm of the relative, where pain, suffering, and individual stories are both natural and palpable. They are to be honored. No one should make light of anyone's experiences. I have not been sex trafficked or raped, nor am I dealing with PTSD. These experiences are not to be discounted; they carry weight and consequences, profoundly affecting the lives they touch.

On the other hand, the realm of the absolute transcends individual and collective narratives. It's a realm where all phenomena are seen as transient, arising and passing away, without an inherent, enduring identity. Both are not mutually exclusive; they exist simultaneously, providing different lenses through which we can experience and interpret reality. Taking the metaphor of a movie: the protagonist's suffering is very real within the confines of the movie's world. Yet, we know it's a scripted narrative that is part of a larger construct. The emotional weight doesn't negate that it's a series of scenes projected onto a screen, built up of frames, lights, and sound. The suffering is real, but it's also a fabrication of storytelling. In the larger construct here, the actor, embodying the protagonist, relishes their role amidst the film's challenges and receives compensation for maintaining the illusion of reality.

By understanding both the relative and the absolute, we can approach life with greater depth where we can be deeply compassionate and present to the suffering in the world while also maintaining a perspective that doesn't get entirely consumed by it. That bridge can be easily seen when we can see the difference between the content of the mind and the perspective of that which sees the content of the mind.

When we shift our focus from the content of the mind to the awareness that sees, the awareness of the Self, a transformative process begins to unfold. Initially, this experience

might feel like inhabiting three distinct realms simultaneously. The first realm is the mental landscape, a space constructed entirely of thoughts. As explained earlier, and I'm sure
you can relate, this realm feels as real as *material reality*, only
without tangible and material substance.

The second realm you begin to perceive is that of sensory
experience. This is where you feel the acute aliveness of your
body: your heart pounding more quickly, your hands becoming somewhat jittery, and your gut experiencing sensations
often categorized as discomfort. Indeed, these are the uncomfortable sensations that many attempt to suppress when
anxiety strikes. However, closer scrutiny reveals that these
sensations are just that—not too dissimilar from those experienced during moments of excitement.

Finally, the third realm you start to tune into is the "real
world," or the plane of objective existence. This realm is composed of consciousness and is, in fact, consciousness itself.
Here, a profound sense of aliveness prevails, one that feels
even more palpable than what's experienced in the other two
realms. This evokes an array of compelling questions: What
is the nature of this experience? Who am I? Eventually, that
last question evolves into an even deeper inquiry: What am
I? At this stage, one becomes keenly aware of observing both
thoughts and bodily sensations. While it becomes clear what
these thoughts imply about one's perceived reality, it remains
an enigma as to who—or what—is the *this* noticing all of it.

In my experience, identifying the illusory patterns of perception invites a kind of stillness. This resembles the situation
of a parched traveler in the desert who spots a mirage. Upon
recognizing the illusion, there's little point in expending energy to chase after the semblance of water. Instead, the wise
course of action is to conserve that energy and simply wait
for genuine nourishment—in this case, rain. But this rain

does not fall. It puddles out of the belly as a river of living water.

No wonder in the writings of the Gospel, according to Matthew, Jesus is [17]written to have said: "*Do not worry about your life, what you will eat, what you will drink nor about your body, what you will put on. Is life more than food and the body more than clothing? Look at the birds of the air, for they neither sow nor reap nor gather into barns, yet the Father feeds them. Which of you by worrying can add one cubit to his stature?*"

Life, you see, is held together so firmly by a mystery that is incomprehensible. With all of our science, we will never get to the bottom of this mystery of aliveness. As science in itself is engulfed by this mystery. It's no wonder we could watch a plant grow; we could talk about the process of growth, but we will never explain consciousness. The entire cosmos is held together by this mystery, and even if this *holding-together* falls, we still will not be able to comprehend it.

What remains constant is this *mystery*. What changes is everything within it. Including emotions. What is the field in which these emotions play? To whom do they affect? Who benefits? Who gains? Are these emotions not a luminous exhibition of grace, a celestial ballet in the theater of human experience? Do they not erupt like a kaleidoscopic cascade of fireworks, each burst a radiant testament to the beauty and complexity of our lives- *Life* itself?

The one who recognizes this flux is a lover of *what is*.

the masseuse's visit

has your masseuse ever told you
about your tense shoulders
how the weight of your world
found home in them?

has your masseuse ever told you
about the knot in your back
how that's the worry about your rent?

drink a lot of water, she says
as you close the door behind you.

nerve us

we don't touch the world, pure and vast,
we filter it through a system.
reality skewed by nerves' own state,
alters the truths we contemplate.

not a direct experience we hold,
but a version our system's framed and told.
thus our view, partial and confined,
is a mirror of the nervous system.

struggles

i was struggling. seriously struggling
i had tried every single thing i knew to try
i had read all the tips and tricks
from the best of gurus
consulted the best of coaches
but i just couldn't change anything.

i didn't want repeat patterns of the past
so i kept trying to avoid the past
i tried everything against it
i fought against it.
i built a bunker in it.
i built traps for all those repeating patterns
it wasn't long before i realized
i had built a comfortable home in the past.

it protected me from the future.
and so my future was the past

i was struggling. seriously struggling
i had tried every single thing i knew to try
i had read all the tips and tricks
from the best gurus
consulted with the best law of attraction maestros
they told me to imagine the future
and through that my reality would change.

so i saved up and invested in the future.
i pushed on. i clenched by butt cheeks
trying to fully visualize with all the strategies
i was given.

it didn't take me long to realize that i no longer
had what it took to see what was right in front of me
the only thing that truly mattered— life itself
unfolding and unfurling every moment.

unknowns

nothing is known
not the future
not the present

nothing is known
not the past
and certainly,
not the present.

love and fear

fear stands clear,
in the shadows, where doubt adheres.
it weaves its webs, intricate and tight,
casting nets of "should" and "might."

love embraces,
in the spaces between breath and phrases.
it paints the sky with hues of grace,
leaving trails that fear can't trace.

fear holds close,
like a vine that chokes the rose.
it grips the heart, saying, "stay or flee,"
in a garden that whispers, "just be."

love holds dear,
what fear claims to revere.
it cradles the moon, the stars, the night,
even the darkness is touched by its light.

fear grasps,
as if life is a task.
it clings to forms, to roles, to names,
yet misses the essence that fuels the flames.

love lets go,
for it's in the letting, we truly grow.
no chains, no bounds, a limitless sea,
in love's embrace, we're forever free.

fear grasps
love lets go.

seeing through anxiety

and so you watch the body contract
at every thought
as consciousness
joyfully latches onto
every idea

you marvel as you notice
every thought was its own making,
invisible, formless, shapeless
like smoke dancing its way
to heaven when the candle is blown out
after all, the fire was real.

and so you watch as the mind flutters
unsure what to do next.
to go left or to go right?
to go up or to go down?
to stay in place or to find a place to stay?
a meaningless game of 'mine'.

but how can the mind know itself?
how can the mirror see itself?
self-help and religion only polish the mirror
gurus and hearsay only glaze the glasses

so we forget the mirrors,
and we forget the reflecting puddles

till we hear the music,
clap to the beat
and so this dance continues
as you watch the body heal.

whole now

we are sufficient.
we are whole.
not later, but now.

thinker to the thought

is there a thinker to the thought,
a sky to the cloud, a seeker to the sought?
the river of mind endlessly flows,
yet who stands apart, nobody knows.

in a theatre of dreams, thoughts put on their play,
stealing the stage, taking the self away.
yet between each act, in the silence so grand,
who lingers there, no script, no plan?

ponder the moon in a puddle's frame
is the reflection separate from the moon's own claim?
thoughts may arise, like waves to the shore,
but where is the ocean when the waves are no more?

we name the unnamable, carving it in parts,
yet it dances as one, in minds and in hearts.
so if thought seeks the thinker, let it journey within,
to find not an answer, but where it's always been.

is there a thinker to the thought?
or is this, too, a notion, endlessly sought?
in this riddle's core, mystery unfolds its art,
the thinker and the thought were never apart.

judgement

what if judgement
came from a place
of insecurity?

thinker to the thought

the universe is
trying to tell you something.
can you hear it?

you are the universe
and your stories are valid,
yet self-created.

running aimlessly

we are so good at running,
we run so much from our pain
that we catch up with what we run from

eventually.

be

you will read a million books
visit a thousand satsangs
consult a 100 teachers
fight 5 or 10 nudges
because you
cannot just
understand
that where
you are
is the
only
place
you
can
be

yesterday

where is yesterday
when the thought
of yesterday is
not here?

7

Resistance and Play

~~~~~~~~~

"See, this is the real secret of life: to be completely engaged with what you're doing in the here and now—and instead of calling it work, realize that this is play"— Alan Watts

White people can't dance!

Have you heard that stereotype being cast? Well, let me let you in on a secret. You'd probably pay to make me stop if you saw me dancing. Or maybe you're the type that would sling out your phone to record my dance moves for a chance to share with the world the rigidity that is this body. You don't understand! I dance like a pencil struggling to bend. I make the robot look like a dance of fluid grace. I dance like a scarecrow in a cornfield, stuck in one pose while the world dances around me. It's easy to troubleshoot my ballroom rigidity.

Dance is an art form that relies heavily on the fluidity of movement. And with any form of stiffness, there's a restriction on the fluidity that is so required in executing moves that require a range of motion. This lack of fluidity can make even simple steps look awkward and forced, detracting from the overall performance. Look, I'm not trying to say that my dance teacher told me I was hopeless. I am just saying there's a story there.

And now you know why a dance teacher I once worked with gave up on me. Well, not quite, but close.

It becomes evident that the stiffness I experience while dancing stems from my body and mind's rigidity rather than allowing for a freedom of movement that is more intuitive and in harmony with music. The root cause hindering the fluidity of my movements is, essentially, resistance. But what exactly constitutes resistance in this context?

The metaphor of simultaneously pressing a vehicle's gas and brake pedals is an apt description of what resistance feels like. In any automotive context, activating the accelerator and brake pedals simultaneously creates a paradox of conflicting commands, which can manifest many complications. These issues can span from accelerated mechanical degradation to critical safety risks.

When both pedals are engaged in a vehicle, the engine receives conflicting commands: one urging acceleration, another insisting on deceleration. This dual signaling not only exerts additional stress on the engine but can also disrupt modern automobiles' sophisticated electronic control systems standards. Over an extended period, such behavior exacerbates wear and tear on critical engine components, escalating maintenance needs.

Doesn't our internal resistance operate in much the same way? You decide to pursue a particular course, only to encounter a conflicting impulse that pulls you in the opposite direction— leaving you paralyzed between the two. Consider a social setting where you aspire to be more outgoing. Yet, you find yourself unable to initiate conversations due to a palpable sense of resistance. Alternatively, you may grapple with the decision to be honest with your partner about a sensitive matter but continuously fail to find the opportune moment or the right words. Similarly, resistance may manifest when you're contemplating standing up for yourself but are uncertain whether such assertiveness is the proper course of action. Or the anticipatory anxiety many experience on a Sunday night when considering the looming Monday.

Resistance often originates from a perceived threat to our "safe zones"—fear of vulnerability, judgment, or significant life changes. Much like fear and anxiety, this is a vestigial response from our evolutionary past, designed to protect us from immediate physical dangers. In today's world, this mechanism is often misaligned with reality.

The antidote to resistance is its direct antithesis—letting go. While this may sound paradoxical, letting go is simultaneously the most challenging and the simplest thing one can do. In truth, the doing is more of a not-doing. When we let go, we relinquish the illusion of control or *doership*, placing our trust in the unfolding process. This trust emanates from a deeply rooted trust that you remain secure regardless of your actions or inactions, largely because it's the mind that dictates the significance—or lack thereof—of events.

However, authentic letting go is seldom experienced without mental subterfuge. The mind has a knack for misinterpreting the act of release as yet another object to cling to.

At first glance, letting go might be misconstrued as complacency, akin to capitulating or even allowing exploitation by others, including oneself. When seen through, it becomes apparent that all of life revolves around releasing resistance. In this state of surrender, there is an intrinsic wisdom that effectively lubricates the gears of resistance. The fall-out is a flavor that feels like play!

When you relinquish even the act of letting go, it's as though the 'self' descends into a dark, profound, seemingly bottomless abyss only to encounter a different kind of illumination. It's in this realm that you uncover the potency and significance of play. Suddenly, the world appears orchestrated—all our challenges, struggles, and preconceptions about life are merely performances on a grand stage, with each individual as a mere actor. When viewed through the lens of play, it becomes evident that in genuinely enjoyable play, there are neither winners nor losers. No one engages in play purely for the sake of a predetermined outcome. The joy is inherent in the act of playing itself. Indeed, the moment the objective of a playful activity shifts toward designating a winner or loser, resistance infiltrates the equation, invariably leading to suffering.

It's striking to observe that our innate affinity for play directly correlates with our capacity for joy and ease in life. The more gravely we approach life, the less room we leave for play, which in turn precipitates a cascade of struggles, sapping the joy out of existence. Thus, the self-perpetuating cycle persists.

In my professional role, I incorporate elements of play into corporate learning environments. The transformative power of playful engagement has proven to be more effective than poring over Excel sheets to dissect workplace chaos and conflict. One of the most profound insights I've gleaned is that adults are essentially children burdened with additional responsibilities and outfitted with a different array of toys. Tragically, many have lost touch with the elemental joy of play.

In your own space, what can you do to turn the most mundane activity to play? You may discover for yourself that nothing was ever that serious. In the unseriousness, work starts to cut like butter.

I am reminded of a passage I read recently in the Chinese classic *Zhuangzi*, that gently shines a light on the contrast between resistance and the lack of it.

"Butcher Ding was cutting up an ox for Lord Wenhui. At every touch of his hand, every heave of his shoulder, every move of his feet, every thrust of his knee—zip! zoop! He slithered the knife along with a zing, and all was in perfect rhythm, as though he were performing the dance of the Mulberry Grove or keeping time to the Ching-shou music.

'Ah, this is marvelous!' said Lord Wenhui. 'Imagine skill reaching such heights!'

Butcher Ding laid down his knife and replied, 'What I care about is the Way, which goes beyond skill. When I first began cutting up oxen, all I could see was the ox itself. After three years I no longer saw the whole ox. And now—now I go at it by spirit and don't look with my eyes. Perception and understanding have come to a stop and spirit moves where it wants. I go along with the natural makeup, strike in the big hollows, guide the knife through the big openings, and following things as they are. So I never touch the smallest ligament or tendon, much less a main joint.

'A good butcher changes his knife once a year—because he cuts. A mediocre Butcher changes his knife once a month— because he hacks. I've had this knife of mine for nineteen years and I've cut up thousands of oxen with it, and yet the blade is as good as though it had just come from the grindstone. There are spaces between the joints, and the blade of the knife has really no thickness. If you insert what has no thickness into such spaces, then there's plenty of room—more than enough for the blade to play about it. That's why after nineteen years the

blade of my knife is still as good as when it first came from the grindstone.

    '*However, whenever I come to a complicated place, I size up the difficulties, tell myself to watch out and be careful, keep my eyes on what I'm doing, work very slowly, and move the knife with the greatest subtlety, until—flop! the whole thing comes apart like a clod of earth crumbling to the ground. I stand there holding the knife and look all around me, completely satisfied and reluctant to move on, and then I wipe off the knife and put it away.*'

    '*Excellent!*' *said Lord Wenhui. 'I have heard the words of Butcher Ding and learned how to care for life!*'

If you can, and if you will, play some really good music, get up on your feet and dance. Really dance! And see for yourself who it is that sees that body? Who is it that notices your sway and swirl? Who is it that witnesses your motion and the thought about the silliness in this moment?

    Who is it, eh?

letting go

letting go
versus letting ego
versus letting god.

english is funny.

resting in resistance

resistance is a tensing against
what you don't prefer
it's an argument with reality

resting in resitance is a paradox
best enjoyed with tea.

being with what is

everything is here now.
it's thoughts that come
into this moment
to contaminate the joy that is

and we can't really think
about thinking about thoughts.

identify, let it go and be with *what is*

when the storms rage
we want to fight with the mind.

source of consciousness

it's hilarious how philosophers
and neuroscientists are scrambling
to understand and explain
the source and cause of consciousness.
consciousness just swinging and swaying
in #thegloriousdance
of losing itself to find itself.
but not ever losing itself
and not ever finding itself.
and not this
also not that.

always whole

in the struggle to hold on
i broke myself apart.

when i let go
i found
each piece was always
whole.

walls grew tall
as i pushed against them.
resisting,
the more i pushed
the less i moved

when i whispered love
to my fears,
my doubts,
my walls,
they folded into petals
leading me
to a garden of self

always waiting
always there
always whole.

solace in these skies

finding solace in moments of sheer liberation
like birds soaring in the skies,
unburdened by attachments, freed from worldly ties.

in the gentle embrace of compassion's wings,
blissful tranquility, the soul sweetly sings,
whispers of impermanence gently remind,
the beauty lies in every moment we find.

so let us dance, like petals in the breeze,
embracing life's wonders, with effortless ease,
for in truth we are whole and not a part,
manifesting divinity, within our humble heart.

what can i compare this to

what can i possibly compare this moment to?
a river's flow, unbroken, yet ever new.
the stillness in the air, before dawn breaks through,
a cosmic dance, where both the one and many brew.

the dissolution of 'me', no subject and no view,
boundaries blurred, distinctions far and few.
the now expands, an endless avenue,
no future to chase, no past to subdue.

here, right and wrong meets its final cue,
a seamless blend of the void and life's hue.
no need to seek, for seeking skews the true,
the present is the lens, both clear and askew.

in this quiet space, wisdom accrues,
god whispers, in silence, its ultimate clue.
the potency of here and now, both the old and the new.

who knew?
who had a clue
that in plain sight
all along was the truth.

freedom's expression

'what brings you fulfillment', she asks.

'oh that's simple. loads and loads of money', i replied.
'so what does the money do?'

'it allows me to travel wherever i want,
buy whatever i want'.

'oh, so i hear a value being communicated.
you mean freedom!
what then does freedom do?
is it not to express the innate aliveness that's within you.
is that expression not the dance of being?'

resistance and love

where ever there's resistance
there's no love?
in what ways can this be true?

what can i compare this to

i find that when we ask the question
"but how do i let go"
there's still resistance.

letting things be
is fully known
when you can see
that your assumed *efforting*
changes nothing,
as things are already what they are.

so, get up and dance!

love, the perfect balm

in the same vein,
love becomes the perfect balm
for every resistance
in what ways can you see love?

evolution

focus on process not outcome!
take a look at the world!
take a look at the universe
it's not done!
it's continuously evolving.
nothing is truly done
but everything evolves.

what sense does it make
longing for what was?

the hyperrealist

the hyperrealist is not thinking
about the eye that she's drawing
she's aware of a pixel,
and another one
and then this one
this one, darker than the other
this one lighter than the next

she's lost in the wonder of hand pressure
and the complex stains of lead
every single dot put in place,
every single line drawn to state.

the hyperrealist is not thinking about the nose
the nose doesn't exist
the eye doesn't exist
there are no skin pores
there are no lip cracks.
there are just lines and spaces
there are just values and shades

you call it a beautiful drawing
awareness moonwalks through
in the mind's illusion.

8

Death, Debt, Barbie and Ken

〜〜〜〜〜〜

"Whoever finds the meaning of these words will not taste death."— *Jesus in the Gospel of Thomas*

In the Barbie movie featuring Margot Robbie, a scene unfolds on the dance floor where Barbie and her friends groove to "Dance The Night" by Dua Lipa. Amidst the pulsating beats and synchronized moves, Barbie initiates a conversation with the other characters on the dance floor.

"Barbie, I feel so beautiful. This is the best day ever, so is yesterday, and so is tomorrow, and so is the day after tomorrow, and even Wednesdays and every day for now until forever. You guys ever thinking about dying?"

The music stops abruptly, and so does the dance. Everyone stares at Barbie with a confused look. Barbie looks at each face with confusion in her eyes and then tries to save the moment,

"I don't know why I said that," she pauses. "I am just... dying to dance!"

And so the music continues.

. . . .

Exploring the subject of death is definitely interesting to dance to— a dark waltz that is both captivating and macabre. Yet, haven't we all died a million deaths? Aren't the thoughts and feelings of death as real to us as the feeling of aliveness — different sides to the same coin of existence?

Have you not noticed that all the flavors of fear we experience are just the fear of physical death itself? Meanwhile, all the love that we feel is of our aliveness. We, therefore, all know what it is to die just the same way living is undeniably our experience. Can't you intuit that you could never die, even if the body dies? Perhaps this exploration would be us biting more than we can chew at this moment. But we will get there!

We'll inevitably confront two kinds of death viscerally. One is the death of the body, and the other is the death of an assumed imagined self. Let's talk about the death of the body for a second.

The death of the body is probably the most certain event that will happen to the human form, yet it is the reality most denied. Mention to someone, "Hey, you're going to die someday," and observe how quickly the conversation shifts. And yet, death's ambush is ever-imminent, looming closer with each tick of the clock. Even as I write this book, I am aware of the limitations and uncertainties that holds this body. Let's face it; The body that holds this book could die before finishing it. Nothing, indeed, is certain. From a biological standpoint, the act of being born sets the stage for our demise. And this paradox warrants contemplation!

Stating that death is an intrinsic aspect of life truly is a darkly comedic paradox, which I know can be met with laughter and seriousness rather than with dread. In this section, I intend to gently grease the resistance behind the thought of death so that we can truly experience life. Or at least marvel at its mystery.

The death of the body is not scary. Perhaps it's our thoughts about death, that is. Likewise, the death of the self/ego/me should not be met with fear but an opportunity to explore what is outside of such a death. Jesus said, "You must lose your life to gain it."

Throughout our lives, we construct identities composed of social norms, personal experiences, and self-perceptions. We become bankers, mothers, artists, and rebels. But at some point, these roles fade or mutate, signifying the death of that particular instance of constructed self. A mother becomes an empty-nester, a daughter becomes a mother, and an artist becomes a corporate salesman—the personas die, but the individual continues. It sometimes takes a midlife crisis or tragic loss to suddenly realize that we build identities behind those roles and claim them to be who we are. A dominant yet subtle voice in our thought structures grabs onto those roles and identities and claims it as *me*. And so when this '*me*' loses hold of something it once claimed as its own, an internal fight erupts. The same mechanism we examined in the chapter, **Resistance and Play**.

Through contemplation, it could be seen that the grasping is imaginary, a colorful illusion. You begin to see that the more the '*me*' grabs onto things, the more unsatisfied it is. The more unsatisfied it is, the more it keeps holding, and this pattern continues until it is fully seen through. When fully seen through, the non-rigidity of this *me* is almost laughable and there lies its death— some may call this *ego death*. The blueprint and typology of this death is seen in physical or cellular death through the lens of a phenomenon called *apoptosis*.

Apoptosis is a process of cellular self-destruction, also known as programmed cell death. It is a crucial mechanism that helps maintain tissue homeostasis and prevent the growth of abnormal or harmful cells. During apoptosis, the cell undergoes a series of changes that can include cell shrinkage, chromatin condensation, and the breakdown of cellular organelles. The process is initiated by various signaling pathways, including the extrinsic and intrinsic pathways critical for development, immune system function, and cancer prevention. Apopstasis selectively removes cells that are harmful or unnecessary. Analogously, as one's experience of a perceived reality begins to dismantle, there is a shedding of entrenched beliefs and self-concepts. This process leads to the collapse of the rigid, constructed self, giving way to life unfolding in its raw form.

Initially, the dissolution of this illusory self can evoke fear. The *me* construct, while potentially limiting, offers a veneer of safety and predictability. When it disintegrates, questions of existential security arise: "Will I be alright without this conceptual self?"

The nun and Christian mystic Bernadette Roberts in her [18]book, *The Path to No-Self,* describes it as "*a movement from an I-thou consciousness to a simple and singular We consciousness. The end of which will be marked by a definitive, unitive revelation: a wholly divine center wherein our deepest self is hidden in oneness with God.*"

As a matter of fascination, the different religious traditions have different expressions for this type of apoptosis. In Buddhism, it's loosely referred to as Awakening. In Hinduism, Moksha. In Taoism, Wu Wei. In Sufism, it's called Fana. In Zen, Satori. In the Kabbalah, it's called Ein Sof, and in Christianity, it's called being born again.

Looking from these various lenses at the same thing, we

can see how apoptosis, whether in the physical body or in a rigid self-referential, reveals that the elimination of certain cells or self-concepts serves as a harbinger of new life or transformation. In this light, the fear traditionally associated with death could be reevaluated. Could we, perhaps, reframe death as a cause for celebration rather than dread?

Artistic mediums like art, literature, and music have long grappled with the concept of death. From the tragic fates of Shakespeare's heroes—Othello, Macbeth, Hamlet, and Romeo— to the elegiac notes of Chopin's funeral marches, these works perform dual roles. They both romanticize death and force us to confront its inevitability, thereby disarming its terror while elevating its poetic dimensions. This cultural treatment turns death into a textured character within our shared narrative, not merely a full stop(or period) at the end of life's sentence.

The act of turning death into a commercialized symbol is also paradoxical. On the one hand, it involves making money from the inevitable, reinforcing a capitalist system where even death becomes a marketplace. On the other hand, commodifying death can also be seen as an acknowledgment of our mortality, a shared recognition of the cosmic irony that surrounds us. In a sense, the commodification of death is an extension of its incorporation into our culture; it is a part of our economic and social lives, as well as our art and philosophies.

What's intriguing is how this commodification process captures another dimension: the material handling of an immaterial, existential issue. Coffins, memorial services, and life insurance are grounded, tangible reactions to the intangible. They're a way to make palpable a concept that is deeply disconcerting and, for some, utterly incomprehensible. In other words, by putting a price tag on death, we're attempting to bring it within the scope of human understanding and control.

The symbiosis between death and economics paints a complex picture. Death, in this view, becomes a form of "debt" owed to the phenomenon of life. This transaction eventually must be "settled." Much like taxes, this debt is inescapable and gives rise to a host of subsequent trades and transactions. The economics of death are as layered as the phenomenon itself, interwoven in a fabric of socio-economic systems that both trivialize and seemingly make monuments of it.

It takes on yet another layer, morphing into a quasi-economic entity—a product to be managed, a debt to be paid, an investment to consider. This layer adds to the complexity and multi-dimensionality of how we perceive and engage with the concept of death- another chapter in the ever-expanding narrative of our collective existence(at least within this mind-created narrative of our collective story).

The death of loved ones serves as a profound catalyst for existential reflection. In the harshest of ironies, it is often through the absence of someone else's physicality that we come to recognize the indivisibility of our own spiritual essence from that of the universe.

It is a revelation steeped in paradox: at the same moment that we acknowledge the unbearable finality of a loved one's absence, we are also awakened to the boundless interconnectedness of all existence. The essence that departs a physical vessel doesn't vanish but rather diffuses, reminding us that our own essence was never compartmentalized to begin with. We're not individual, isolated entities; we're part of a unified field of consciousness, a mosaic of *beingness* that transcends the boundaries of flesh and bone.

This experience does not negate the pain of loss. Still, it adds a transformative layer to it, a deeper understanding that taps into the nondualistic nature of reality. While the corporeal form is gone, the essential nature it manifested has simply rejoined the greater pool of consciousness. In other words, the absence created by loss is a vivid reminder of an all-encompassing presence. By forcing us to confront our own mortality and the fragility of our physical existence, the death of a loved one compels us to reevaluate not only our relationship with the departed but our relationship with existence itself. Far from rendering our individual essence incomplete, this confrontation with loss catalyzes a more comprehensive realization of our integral nature within the greater web of existence.

Death is both the most natural and the most extraordinary event we'll experience. Far from being taboo, it deserves to be contemplated, studied, even celebrated. It's a rite of passage, a universal experience, and an intricate part of the human narrative. Our relationship with death can be seen as a complex ballet, full of contradictions and ironies. But as we dance this mysterious waltz, we can be reminded that death itself is only an imagined transitional gate. In the transitions, in the cross between an assumed life of the constructed self, a new dimension of being emerges—the true Self. In this emergence is the death of *what was*. "[19]*Old things have passed away and all things have become new*". The past becomes the meaningless back story of a fictitious character, the future, a dream imagined, and the Self unbound by conditioning or experience; it is the observer of such experiences and yet not different from the experiences. It exists in an untainted state of freedom. Well, it does not exist at all. All things exist from it.

~~~~~~~~~~~~~~~~~~~~

Barbie to Ken, "You have to figure out who you are. You're not your girlfriend, you're not your house, you're not your mink. You're not even Beach. Maybe all the things you thought made you YOU aren't ...really you".

In an instance of realization, Ken shouts in pure joy, "Ken is me! Ken is me! Ken is me".

The other Kens, also waking up to their true identity, respond, "We were only fighting because we didn't know who we are."

a taste of eden

who told you you were naked?
"it was the serpent!" you declare.
yet in the whisper of leaves,
a different tale unfurls in eden's air.

here, the tree of life sways, not bound by sin or lore,
its roots deep in the soil, its branches aiming more.
a fruit so sweet, it sings, of freedom ever pure,
one taste and see—you are the garden,
nothing less, nothing more.

the leaves don't question if they're worthy of the sun,
nor does the bloom seek judgment for its hue.
the fruit falls, not pondering if it's the chosen one,
for here, in eden's grace, division is undone.

so take a bite, my love, let life's juice stain your soul,
in this sacred space, you're neither part nor whole.
you are, and always were, the story and the scroll,
a single taste reveals—you're both the seer and the seen.

imagination and the body

instead of imagining,
maybe focus on living

in this body.

in this moment.

am i alive?

this aliveness
this aliveness
this aliveness
before the stories start

this aliveness
this aliveness
this aliveness
with all the story lines

am i alive?
is the answer not.

all is yours

blind to all you lack,
you see clearly that
all is yours.

your last breathe

your last breathe
would be an out breathe
one of letting go
of all that you had
or thought you had.

all that you had inhaled
and held onto

your last breathe
will precede
the inhaling of a new realization
all you ever were was unseen
a formless essence
free from the clutches
of pain and suffering.

there will be no more tears
all will be known
as you are known

your next breathe will be yours to hold.

the parts of us

there's a part of us
that cannot be tarnished
by our ruminations,
by actions against us
a part that is alive and only alive
it's never died and will never die
it's the one we can know but can't be seen
the part that sees the one that knows
that part is all parts
soprano, alto, tenor and bass
it's the harmony and the discord
it's the length, breath and the measureless
it's formless but yet informed
it's shapeless yet shapes eternity
it is the i that's dancing to it's own song.

the sun

how can we see
that the ray of sunlight
and the sun are the same thing.
how can we see
that the sun is self-illuminating
and it's ray illuminated
by nothing but itself.

melchizedek

i will not be. i was not. i am.
in this moment's breath, eternity's span.

like a phoenix, i'm both ash and flame,
neither bound by future, nor tethered by name.

time's illusion crumbles, a ticking, hollow scam.
in the stillness, i find no line or diagram.

i will not be. i was not. i am.
a fleeting whisper in the cosmic program.
in this now, both the questioner
and the examination.

i will not be. i was not. i am.

melchizedek.

death and life

if we would only wake up
to the realization
that life and death
are of the same coin.

as you die, you live.
as you live you die.
death, the beginning of life;
life the beginning of death.

human

"but we are human" —
as if being human is a weakness.
"but we are all human" —
as if being human is a mistake.

as if being human
is not to transcend
who you thought you were— human.

transcending human.

no life

shedding all attachments
i am only attached to life
not that there could ever be one

there is no life,
yet we call it life.

new beginnings

have you heard
that new beginnings
are sometimes
disguised as painful endings?

walking dead

If you can't be found
in your body
then nobody
is their body.

where are they?

9

The Problem with Problems

~~~~~~~~~~~~~~~~

"If we think there is a problem with the world, we have a problem! Life is a celebration"
— Francis Lucille

A bat and ball together cost $1.10. The bat costs $1.00 more than the ball. What is the cost of the ball?

If your initial answer is $1, you're incorrect, like 90% of individuals who first tackle this mathematical conundrum. While a detailed exploration of the cognitive biases or short-comings that lead to such frequent mistakes lies beyond the scope of this chapter, a quick Google search will elucidate both the correct answer and the flaws in your reasoning.

To tantalize you further, consider this: The answer is so glaringly obvious, and yet we may still spend minutes puzzling over its correctness even when it's laid out before us. This principle extends to every problem we encounter in life. Sometimes, the solutions are unintuitive yet true; at other times, they're self-evident. Then there are dilemmas with answers that are categorically elusive, though we might not recognize them as such. Regardless, it may be beneficial to perceive each problem akin to a crossword puzzle—existing for its own intrinsic value, for its own pleasure, independent of the solution.

Everything, without exception, serves as a symbol and expression of the divine. Even the dirt on the floor and situations that seem to be falling apart are manifestations of the divine. Depending on how you see it, this may sound crazy. But here is the thing: examine everything called a 'problem'. What are they made of? Where do they exist? Whether sensed, seen, or perceived, they seem to emanate from thought. If seen through, you'd recognize thought is energy. All phenomena, therefore, are expressions of the inherent perfection of being.

It's easy to recognize this perfection in aesthetically pleasing things—gorgeous flowers, breathtaking landscapes, and so on. But what about dilapidated houses, wars, or our personal struggles? Nothing can truly be separated; it's all part of an intricate, interdependent system.

To label things as problems, evil, sacred, or holy is merely to engage in narrative-spinning, fabricating stories about a system of reality that is fundamentally unfathomable. Our judgments of what's good or bad have no impact on the fundamental nature or the ongoing operations of the system of existence. This system is perpetually unfolding; you are an inextricable part of it.

So, any narrative we construct is just that—a construct. These stories can't alter the intrinsic nature of existence; at most, they can only distort our perception of it. Labeling things as 'problems' or categorizing them as 'good' or 'bad' is a conceptual overlay that obscures the fundamental nature of *what is*. The act of naming things as separate entities allows for judgments of value to be applied. However, their inherent nature remains unchanged regardless of how we label or categorize things.

Naming each wave doesn't separate them from the ocean—they are still expressions of a more extensive, unified system. They result from a complex interaction of oceanic currents, wind forces, gravitational pulls, temperature, and the prevailing conditions at that particular moment.

None of this says that problems shouldn't be looked into; the focus here is on transforming our relationship with what we identify as problems. To truly understand the nature of a problem, one must scrutinize not only the problem itself but also the mental framework in which it is couched. Break down the constituents of the thoughts that define the problem. Examine the components that make up the 'self' you believe is entangled in the situation. This kind of investigation offers new perspectives, potentially leading to novel and more effective solutions for what initially seemed problematic.

Remember, the categorization of a situation as a "problem" stems from one's own mental framing. Ironically, you cannot definitively assert that something is a problem. Situations have intractable complexities, eluding even the most nuanced conceptual frameworks. Regardless of how sophisticated our thoughts may be, they are inherently limited. In contrast, the essence of any situation is boundless and interwoven with endless variables and implications. Thus, our finite cognition can never fully encapsulate the infinite complexities of reality.

The person with a problem is not the 'one' who is seeing and experiencing the constructed persona. I know this could sound confusing to some. To elucidate, consider this: there is an awareness of the character undergoing a particular circumstance or issue. It may sound like a form of dissociation, but it's an important distinction to grasp. The "human be-ing"—the protagonist, if you will—in your lived experience is often about succeeding or failing. But there's an awareness that neither needs to succeed nor fail; its victories or defeats are irrelevant. That's because the character, the *human*, isn't really "you." You are, in fact, this perfectly clear, indepen-dent, unchanging consciousness that merely observes all these events without reaction. The genre of the life event—be it comedic or tragic—has no bearing on this observer con-sciousness.

The mistake takes root when we identify with the roles we assume, akin to mistaking ourselves for a character in a film who is embroiled in some kind of crisis. A more apt comparison might be to a character in one's dream. While dreaming, you may perceive this character as yourself, nav-igating a labyrinth of challenges and conflicts. Yet, once we change how we awaken, we see and recognize the illusory nature of the dream; the weight of those challenges often dissolves into absurdity.

Upon this realization, you come to understand that you have always been whole and complete. Although the external circumstances may remain the same, your perspective on them undergoes a transformative shift. You're no longer en-tangled in the narrative; instead, you become the conscious observer, free from the limitations imposed by a script you never wrote. A script that plays out of its own accord.

This mode of perception resembles observing a lenticular print. From one vantage point, you discern one image, shift your perspective, and an entirely different scene comes into focus.

What about the act of controlling circumstances, employ-ing tools like the Law of Attraction and other frameworks designed to transform challenges? You might think that manipulating these variables gives you control. However, the illusion of control and the actual state of being in control or not are not caused by singular separate situations. This is a natural outgrowth of the ever-unfolding reality that governs the way we perceive our environment. In essence, it's not so much about the strategies we use to 'solve problems' but rather how those strategies fit into a much larger, interconnected system of being.

You see, the reality is, whether you ever felt in control or not, you were never the root cause of either state. The energies that have shaped your identity, including your entire life history, are accountable for those circumstances—even this is just a story. What you witness is merely a manifestation of the universe's natural unfolding—of reality taking its course.

In any deep exploration of our experiences, scrutinizing our identification with the body and the mind becomes crucial. When we question what we define as 'problems,' it becomes apparent that various mental and biological processes are at play. We can examine how we identify with the body and how we identify with the mind. Neither of them is you, and neither are done by you. Yet you are being done. With that recognition, you can see that every problem is called a problem by a confluence of familiar cognitive activities that we collectively refer to as 'thoughts'. Sometimes, it's interesting to see how shifting our perspectives and how we see can lead to a transformation of thoughts, and when those thoughts change, so does what we once perceived as a problem. In this, I am in no way advocating for one to change their thoughts. The bulk of the Self-help industry advocates for this. It is seen here as purely illusory— you cannot change a thought. In what ways can a 'person' change a thought? However, when we broaden our awareness or shift our perspective, thoughts often seem to evolve autonomously, of their own accord. When our thoughts shift from the assertion of a particular outcome with the given problem to focusing on being, seeing the arising of the 'problem thought' or 'problem situation' as just that, then in a certain way that is indescribable with words, there seems to be an enjoyment of the process that unfolds. This may be described as the *'peace that surpasses all understanding'*. It can be described as happiness— one that's not attached to any outcome for its fulfillment.

I recently learned about an unconventional dining establishment in Japan known as the Restaurant of Mistaken Orders. Remarkably, all the servers at this restaurant have dementia, which results in a 37% error rate in the orders. In practical terms, if you order noodles, you stand an almost 37% chance of being served miso soup instead. Despite this, the establishment has found that the vast majority of its patrons—99%, to be exact—leave the restaurant in a state of happiness, indicating a collective preference for contentment over the precise fulfillment of their orders.

In actuality, this restaurant, set up to create awareness of dementia, subverts the usual expectations about service quality, turning a "mistake" into an experience that jolts people out of routine and forces them to engage with the present moment with empathy and enjoyment.

We could take a cue from this to shift our focus from rigid expectations to fluid experiencing. Many people view problems as mismatches between their expectations and reality. By embracing uncertainty and expecting deviations, these so-called problems can instead be seen as part of the overall experience. The journey becomes the goal. The process becomes the destination.

Is this not what a glorious dance is?

no problem, no solution

when we realize
there's no problem,
what's left is the solution.

if there's no problem,
what's the solution then?

good question.
there was no problem
so there was no solution.

no problem, no solution

whatever changes cannot be eternal,
whether it be days, seasons,
thoughts, the body or the mind.
so also sensations, concepts and beliefs,
this page and the next page.

as being

it is not the uttering of a word that defines us,
but the space left in its wake.
projections are mere echoes in this silence,
fading ripples in an endless sea.
in the silence after, we find a home
that asks for no articulation—
just the unspoken, unfathomable sense
of being and not being.

as being!

painting the unnamed

how often do we paint the unnamed
with the palette of our expectations,
diluting mystery with definition.
yet in the still moments between breaths,
between the projections and the persona,
we glimpse the unnamed, unshamed—
wondrously free of all we thought it was.

the soul dances naked

in the theater of the world,
we dress the stage with our desires.
yet, strip away the costumes and props,
and the soul dances naked,
unburdened by name or form.

sailing

we sail the ocean, storms and wind,
yet yearn for a stillness we find within.
drop the anchor, cease the quest—
you are the ocean, calm and restful.

seeds we sow

like a delicate lotus in serene bloom,
we navigate life's fleeting room,
each breath, a whisper of eternity's touch,
in this ephemeral dance, we find so much.

sunsets paint our souls with colors divine,
awakening wisdom, as dreams intertwine,
just as rivers merge and find their flow,
unity abounds, in the seeds we sow.

time

time is a word of poetry
we took a little too seriously.
now we believe it.

the player and the played

my heart bleeds with pain
as i trudge through the difficulties of life
my veins feel the weight
my bones quiver and shudder
even my eyes see no more color
just grayscale and impending doom
i have prayed to god
but only silence responds
i have asked the whiskey for help
it responded with only a horrible
taste in my mouth.
i have tried watching comedy shows
but i don't hear a word of a joke cracked
apart from the crackling of my own fears
who is the world crumbling for?
the character or the content?
the noticed or the noticer?
the played or the play?

midnight's cloak

midnight's cloak is your backdrop,
a dark embroidery against which your form emerges
like a wraith of light.
the room is still, but you break its silence
with a language only your limbs can speak.
feet gliding over forgotten echoes,
you're a comet tracing invisible orbits in the emptiness.
with every turn, you unravel chains of thought,
letting them disperse like stardust
across the black void of the room.
your dance is an enigma,
a labyrinthine riddle spun in real-time.
the quietude amplifies each motion,
as if your solitude were a magnifying lens
focusing the world's beauty through form.
in this enclosed space, you're not confined
but set free—each stretch,
each jump a boundless expedition
into the landscapes of your inner cosmos.

until now

you've known you all along
you've seen you all along
you just didn't know it was you
until now.

and we are it

could our perception of a broken world
be our internal projection on to an 'external world'?
the mistake- the illusion of us being separate
from this singularity
may be responsible for our insistence

that we are better than,
that they are worse than

without us seeing that the universe is living.
it is constantly healing itself
through us because
and we are it.

10
I Don't Know

~~~~~~~~~

"Everyone sees the unseen in proportion to the clarity of their heart" —
Rumi

Boy, oh boy! You have reached the end of this book and will soon be met with something paradoxical yet anticlimactic. And it's this: I don't know anything. Everything I have written about is just words. Not Truth! Not knowledge and certainly not wisdom.

Maybe you've not read the other parts of this book but somehow found yourself reading just this chapter; you read it right: I really don't know anything.

One evening, I was taking a walk with Milo when it suddenly hit me! There's *nobody* inside of this 'here.'

I froze! Biologic reactions in a body. Mental activities in a concept called mind. *Who the heck is this one that's looking at this body?* It was clear. I could see clearly now! There's *nobody* inside of anybody. There's just a spontaneous, unexplainable play of mind that animates what we see as characters and trees. There's no future, there's no past, there's even no pres-

ent. It all looks like a dream. A lucid dream. For this character, it sometimes appears as a nightmare and sometimes a
dream of Cotton Candyland. Irrespective, it is a mysterious
dream of Oneness. A dream that is apparently happening,
yet I don't know what or how it's happening. It clearly isn't
happening to or for anyone.

I saw what actual freedom was. This is the salvation
talked about in the Christian texts! *This! This is it!* I was eager
to share this profound insight. With enthusiasm, I would
proclaim to all willing to lend an ear that there is *no person*
inside anyone. "Oh god, that doesn't even make sense when
spoken out loud." I anticipated the puzzled looks and vacant
expressions that would inevitably meet my gaze, a response I
could understand. Had I been in their position, I would have
likely dismissed my own words as the ramblings of a mad-
man. I was fully aware of how outlandish my 'revelations'
might seem to anyone. Yet, the lucidity of my understanding
was overwhelming! How could I possibly articulate this new-
found clarity? It was a revelation so vivid and so transformative that finding words to do justice to its magnitude seemed
almost beyond the realm of possibility.

I have listened to tens and tens of people who seem to
know things. I have heard about people who have had mystical experiences; some had apparent conversations with God,
some were just born with the greatest insights, and somehow,
they seem to be pointing to the same things and oftentimes
different things. But there, seeing for oneself is something
that cannot be told.

I invite you to delve into your own inquiry, arm yourself
with more questions, and see that the answers are probably
not the most important things.

I will say this, though: what I express here are words that
come from what I have seen for myself. Even if these words

resonate with words others may have shared, does that mean I or similar thinkers are seeing right?

Like any type of sight, we may all be seeing similar things or totally different things. That you and I are staring at the same ball doesn't mean we see the same ball. You may be seeing a baseball, and I may see a ball with stitches. Same object, different 'seeing.' What philosophers like to call the "incommensurability of subjective experiences." Ultimately, one thing is undeniably true of both experiences. There's the experience of seeing what is happening in both situations. This underscores the idea that while the content of experience may be infinitely variable, the basic structures—like perception, sensation, and emotion—are universal. These are the common 'touch points' of human experience. In Eastern philosophical terms, it's the difference between *nama* (name, form, concept) and *rupa*(essence, experience.) While the names and forms might differ, the essence of the experience—conscious awareness—remains constant.

In seeing, I can simply realize that what's being seen is not as important as seeing itself. I can talk about Truth but Truth is never and will never be in the words spoken. So then, what is Truth?

The answer seems both frighteningly and exhilaratingly obvious. Beyond being the object of universal human quest, Truth is also the one thing toward which all expression inherently gravitates and finds joy. In its most primal form, Truth is fundamental and glaringly evident—or should I say, it is 'nothing' at all.

I often hear assertions like, "Life is merely a hologram or a simulation," or "Perhaps we are all dreaming." These statements hold Truth; maybe they don't. Similarly, some claim that a divine reckoning is imminent, positing that people will either ascend to heaven or descend to hell. Again, maybe that's accurate, maybe not. However, the unquenchable thirst for certainty often blinds us to a nuance we might otherwise perceive. This drive for definitiveness obscures other valuable dimensions of understanding, potentially preventing us from seeing what is plainly right here in front of us.

Truth!

It's the most obvious thing ever! Yet the most elusive! Truth is *this*!

No, not that sentence you just read. Not your conception of it. Not what you're visualizing or imagining. It is this— right here, right now. Do you see it? It's *this*!

Milo, my doggie roommate, provides an apt metaphor for the human condition. Just like he focuses on my finger when I point, instead of understanding that I'm directing his attention to something else, we often fixate on the superficial aspects of Truth without grasping its fundamental essence. We discourse on it, sermonize about it, and discuss those who claim to have discovered it. Yet, we overlook what is glaringly apparent right in front of us. Analogous to a fish that swims in water yet can't perceive it, we exist in a state of Truth that's so inherent to our being, so immediate, that we fail to recognize it. Indeed, Truth is closer to us than anything else, but recognition is essential.

Ever engaged in a frantic search for a pen—checking under tables, rifling through bags, leafing through books, scanning shelves, and even questioning those around you—only to realize you were holding it the entire time? That's what this revelation feels like. Despite my throwing words on this page about Truth, expressing how obvious it is, it is what I have been hinting at all along.

My understanding of what Truth is has become increasingly apparent. Moreover, this understanding brightens with each passing day. As the essence of Truth becomes more evident, all other considerations fall away, leading me to the startling realization that I truly know nothing(I am the darling Jon Snow). To the dualistic mind, this might prompt the question, "What on earth are you talking about? Are you saying you don't know anything else, not even a single thing?"

Yes, you heard correctly.

Here's a pointer: *What is undeniably true?*
Do you see it yet?
Here's another pointer: There is an awareness of your current experience. Perhaps you hear a passerby giggling. You may feel the texture of this page as you read or hold this book. You're currently aware of this. Now, outside of the external experiences, what are you aware of?

Around this point, you may ask who or what is aware of this experience. What is that? This open awareness, what is that?

What is true about awareness?

I don't know anything. I observe experiences unfolding even as I recognize an underlying stillness that suggests nothing is actually happening. It becomes increasingly clear that every assertion can be negated, except for this fundamental Truth: you are that Truth.

I am Truth.

I am.

I am I.

I.

the less you know

this is not happening
and yet it is.
it can't be talked about
and cannot be grasped.
these words don't matter.
yet they matter the most.
there's no us
but only you.
there's no this.
and so no that,
no tit, for no tat.
it's absurd
and linguistically confusing.
if you know this,
the less you know.

dance of love and fear

love and fear
dance in harmony
with each other...
and that's not a bad thing.

who said it was a good thing?

all that ever is.

the inherent trap
is in the identification
of any word as truth,
as if words aren't thoughts
as if thoughts aren't a signal
of the hitch hiker drawing your attention
to *what is.*
truth is all that ever is.
not a fragment of each.
but in all things. all things.

comparison

we suffer when we compare
'what is' to 'what could be'
and even worse, 'what should be'.

in that suffering
we don't see the infinite possibilities
that may come out of 'what already is'

this sounds like hope
but it's only hopeless.

seeking

i know it's been said to
'seek and you will find'.
maybe we need to stop seeking
because we are already found
right here.

not like there's a place called here.

when the spirit moves

when the spirit moves
it moves the body,
moves events
and moves circumstances
synchronicities are unfolded
and the mind is held aghast

when the spirit uncovers it's nakedness
it is seen that neither the body
the events nor the circumstances
were ever removed from it's intimate dance.

i don't know

it doesn't matter what i know,
i still don't know
it just matters that i love you.
that i truly do

in this, i have had no option.
my hatred was love distorted
and my love was love corrected.

and if you don't love me back
it doesn't matter.

coming and going

coming and going,
here and there,
alive and dead,
it's all a dance

appearances
experiences
don't they come
don't they they go

real and not real,
solid and not solid,
here and not here.

is this not marvelous?
is this not the dance of a skillful ballerina?

when we remain still

when we remain still
not pushing away what we do not want
and chasing after what we want
we begin to notice something obvious
the ebbs and flow of life that's so natural
so much so, what we want or don't want
become irrelevant.

god's only hobby

each star a verse,
in the fabric of space,
quantum strings strumming,
cosmic rehearse.
black holes keep secrets,
a mute, silent curse,
time weaves lines,
 in the universe's purse.

atoms rhyme with photons,
a quantum couplet,
dark matter's prose
no instrument can trumpet.
neutrinos dash like metaphors,
so subtle yet fleet,
infinite stanzas in galaxies,
where physics and fancy meet.

ah! god's only hobby is poetry.

Acknowledgments

Acknowledgements

To Jamie Picciarelli. Your love is a constant reminder to me of how to love. The chapter on forgiveness and forgetting was brought about by contemplations on forgiveness after the series of challenges we faced. I can't thank you enough for all the support and the love you show me. Love is stupid, you know. Love, in its inherent irrationality, is precisely what imbues it with its sublime beauty.

To Steve Silbert, for the countless moments we've exchanged thoughts, sketch notes, and verses from the Torah. A particular conversation in the Scrum Room on the 13th floor led me down a thought-provoking path that contributed significantly to this journey. Our visits to the synagogue have consistently been an awe-inspiring experience for me. You have no idea how much it changed the way I saw things. The chapter on Resistance and Play mirrors our continuous exploration of play as a transformative tool in coaching. Your influence, coaching and mentorship has been invaluable, Steve.

To Brian Tom O'Connor, thank you for introducing me to the Awareness Games. These seemingly playful activities in your book provide profound insights into the illusions of perception, and they were mind-opening in the literal sense. Your book was a key inspiration for the chapter on Resistance and Play.

To Matthew Maxwell. I can now hold a cockroach! That I would read your book at the reception of my colonoscopy procedure made me realize I was The Boy! Synchronicities, they say! Thank you!

To Dakota Minnie Boyer, I extend my deepest appreciation for your meticulous attention to the finer details of this project, areas where my abilities and patience are limited. Your generosity is deeply touching. Additionally, your steadfast advocacy for those without a voice and your commitment to the marginalized and oppressed are both commendable and inspiring.

To my dad, whose death, in many ways, gave us life. I write here things you already know. And to you, Mom, see! I paid attention in literature class! The pointers in this book are potent in the revelation of Truth. Explore with me!

Uncle Yomi, thanks for being an ear I can bounce ideas on. Too much to talk about with this one!

To Marian Howard, thank you for fueling my passion for watercolor artistry. This medium has provided me with serene moments where I can contemplate. I hold dear the letters you write me, and I hope in some way the words in this book spark something.

And finally, to my friends who have patiently endured my fervent sharing of these indescribable realizations—Oge Ohaeto, 'Delani, Simone, Jasmine Richmond, Blake, Kay, Princewill Ejirika,Niemah, Dan Bracewell, Fu'ad Lawal, Mounica Chenne, Wunmi Akinde, Simisola Olorunkosebi, Inemesit, Sadie Travis(OMG! I see thoughts!), Linda Maidment, Alyssa Leslie, Lena Shaqareq—your tolerance and understanding when I express these thoughts mean the world to me. The joy I feel knowing these reflections resonate one way or the other and synchronously is immense. It is so obvious that our lived experiences are so different, yet at the core, we have never ever been separate.

To my Father, who I am. It's a glorious ~~joke~~ dance!

References

1   Mark 10:18 NIV

2   Our Real Home. A Talk to an aging lay disciple approaching Death, Ajaan Chah. Translated by The Sangha at Wat Pah Nanachat

3   Ecclesiastes 1:2

4   How Emotions Are Made: The Secret Life of the Brain by Lisa Feldman Barrett.(Mariner Books, January 2018)

5   Libet, Benjamin W. (1999). Do we have free will? Journal of Consciousness Studies 6 (8-9):47-57.

6   On the Phenomenology of the Consciousness of Internal Time (1893–1917) (Husserliana: Edmund Husserl – Collected Works, 4)

7   John 17:16

8   Luke 15:11-32

9   John 17: 21-23 NIV

10 Matthew 25:35-40

11 Matthew 5:24

12 Matthew 18:21-25

13 Luke 6:38

14 The Heart of Who We Are: Realizing Freedom Together(Sounds True. November 2022

15 The Four Agreements: A Practical Guide to Personal Freedom(A Toltec Wisdom Book)(Amber-Allen Publishing. November 1997)

16 Hebrews 4:13

17 Matthew 6:25-30

18 The Path to No-Self: Life at the Center, State University of New York Press

19 2 Corinthians 5:17

Further Readings

The books listed below have proven to be exceptionally potent in their ability to elucidate the essence of our true nature(provided you read between the lines). Each of them provides profound insights, guiding readers on a journey to deeper exploration and understanding.

- Awareness Games: Playing with Your Mind to Create Joy by **Brian Tom O'Connor**(Slippery Mind, 2016).
- Awake: It's Your Turn by **Angelo Dilullo**, (SimplyAlwaysAwake.com, 2021).
- How To Hold A Cockroach: A book for those who are free and don't know it by **Matthew Maxwell**(Hearthstone, 2020).
- The Universal Christ: How a Forgotten Reality Can Change Everything We See, Hope For, and Believe by **Richard Rohr**(Convergent Books, 2019).
- The Naked Now: Learning To See As the Mystics See by **Richard Rohr**(The Crossroad Publishing Company, 2009).
- The Heart of Who We Are: Realizing Freedom Together by **Caverly Morgan**(Sounds True, 2022).
- The Well of Being: A Children's Book for Adults by **Jean-Pierre Weill** (Flatiron Books, 2016).
- I am Always I by **Rupert Spira and Zuzanna Cele-j**(whitefox Publishing Ltd, 2023).
- Being Aware of Being Aware by **Ruper Spira**(Sahaja, 2017).

Table of Contents

About the Author

Seye Kuyinu is a multifaceted character whose diverse passions paint the portrait of a curious individual. His professional role as an Agile Coach is complemented by his creative endeavors and interest in hypnotherapy as a tool to demystify our personal stories. Residing in Jacksonville, Florida, Seye approaches coaching not merely as a vocation but as an exploratory journey into the systems of individuals, teams, organizations, and the stories we tell about them.

Fueled by the realization that certainty is an illusion, his creative endeavors in music, photography, and watercolor art and a deep engagement in hypnotherapy are not just hobbies but extensions of his inquisitive nature. Each medium to this character offers a unique lens through which to examine and express Truth. With hypnotherapy, Seye employs his insights to tap into the structures and limitations of the finite mind, leading to what could be called transformative experiences.

Seye Kuyinu invites you into his world of exploration and discovery through his website, seyekuyinu.com, and his coaching outfit, highlifer.co. Each platform is a gateway to understanding the multifaceted nature of his work and the profound insights he brings to his diverse fields of expertise.

www.ingramcontent.com/pod-product-compliance
Lightning Source LLC
Chambersburg PA
CBHW011234120626
46549CB00009B/3272